#1037

THE ENORMOUS EXCEPTION

THE ENORMOUS EXCEPTION

MEETING CHRIST IN THE SERMON ON THE MOUNT

Earl F. Palmer

WORD BOOKS
PUBLISHER
WACO, TEXAS

A DIVISION OF
WORD, INCORPORATED

Library of Congress Cataloging-in-Publication Data
Palmer, Earl F.
    The enormous exception.

    Bibliography: p.
    1. Sermon on the mount—Commentaries.   I. Sermon on
the Mount.   II. Title.
BT380.2.P26   1986   226'.906   86–9103
ISBN 0–8499–0535–4

67898BKC987654321
Printed in the United States of America

To Anne
daughter and friend

Contents

Right in the middle of all these things stands up an enormous exception. It is quite unlike anything else. It is a thing final like the trump of doom, though it is also a piece of good news, or news that seems too good to be true. It is nothing less than the loud assertion that this mysterious maker of the world has visited his world in person.

Gilbert Keith Chesterton
The Everlasting Man

PREFACE

This book is a twentieth-century commentary on the Sermon on the Mount, but it is more than that for me. It is something of a journal of my own pilgrimage with Jesus the man and Jesus the preacher, as that pilgrimage is focused and intensified by the event and the speech we call the Sermon on the Mount. Jesus' sermon has usually had that effect upon anyone who hears it; and since each new generation of men and women listens to the sentences from the possibilities of different experiences and different vantage points, there is the need in each generation for yet another reflection upon what the sermon means for our lives here and now.

I have been working on this commentary for a long time, and I am grateful to the people in my life and ministry who have endorsed me in this task. I especially appreciate the encouragement I received from Denny Rydberg who invited me to write a commentary in brief on the Sermon on the Mount for the David C. Cook *Lifestyle* series. That special study was my own first attempt at a theological commentary on the text. I also am thankful to my New College Berkeley class where I taught the Sermon on the Mount during the spring semester in 1984. I am grateful to my congregation and staff colleagues at First Presbyterian Church of Berkeley where I serve as pastor, and to my typist, Mary Philips, who is much more than a manuscript typist; she has also been a very helpful editorial critic for me. Finally, thanks also to my family—Shirley, Anne, Jon, and Elizabeth—who support me not only as a pastor trying to write and be a pastor, but more than that, as husband, father, and friend.

Earl F. Palmer
Berkeley, California

INTRODUCTION

"Seeing the crowds, he went up on the mountain, and when he sat down, his disciples came to him. And he opened his mouth and taught them, saying:" (Matt. 5:1, 2).

What a teacher Jesus is! His opening sentences are exciting and baffling all at once. He says things that catch us off guard, and yet because of that, what he says is vivid and unforgettable. For any teaching to make a lasting impression upon our minds, it must include that exciting mixture of things both hard to understand and things easy to understand. The single line in the first inaugural address of Franklin D. Roosevelt, on March 4, 1933, that is most unforgettable is also the line that is not immediately obvious and plainly understandable. The President said to his fellow Americans, "Let me assert my firm belief that the only thing we have to fear is fear itself. . . ." The sentence is powerfully communicative and yet there is a hidden, baffling quality about those words that forces the listener to wonder about all of the possibilities of fear and hope that are present in the sentence. When Jesus tells the distinguished Pharisee Nicodemus "You must be born again" (John 3), we encounter the electrifying power of plain words easy to understand mixed with baffling possibilities in the one sentence. We know what he is saying and yet we do not really know all that he is saying. The implications of what his words mean go far beyond the first thoughts that come into our minds. It is this very exciting mixture of straightforwardness and mystery that describes the Sermon on the Mount.

The words that Jesus uses are simple, straightforward, and familiar. But still, each sentence takes us by surprise. We never would have thought, for example, that the word *happy* might fit with the word *mourn*.

As we begin this study let's ask some questions about the setting for this sermon. Where did this event take place? Who were the listeners? Did Matthew record everything that Jesus said? Is the sermon a single teaching event or a collection of sayings taken from many teaching events?

This incident probably took place near the town of Capernaum. We discover from a comparative reading of the four Gospels that Jesus received his most enthusiastic response from the people of Capernaum, and most of the Galilean ministry that we know about in the New Testament records took place at or near this lakeside village.

It is difficult for us to know how many people Matthew intended by his use of the words "disciples" and "crowd" in his opening sentences. But we can say that "when he sat down" means that the listeners were prepared to hear the words of a rabbi in the place of authority. In rabbinical tradition, the phrase "he sat down" has authoritative significance. It was customary out of respect for the written words of the Old Testament for a rabbi to stand while reading the text, but since in Jewish rabbinical tradition the sermon of the rabbi was not in the tradition of public oration but rather that of teaching and explanation, the rabbi would sit during his exposition. He was thereby *under* the Word and yet the rabbi held borrowed authoritative influence in that he was explaining God's holy will as written in the Law, the Prophets or the Writings. (See Norval Geldenhuys's discussion in his commentary on the teaching of Jesus in the synagogue of Nazareth in Luke 4: *Commentary on the Gospel of Luke.*)

Does Matthew record everything that Jesus said on each subject contained in the sermon? Involved in this question is the matter of the timing. In other words, do we have a collection of teachings from Jesus over a period of time or is the text of Matthew 5–7 a single teaching event? Certainly each of the Gospel writers compressed dialogue and event narration, just as any news reporter must do.* John tells his readers that all of the books of the world could not contain a record of everything Jesus said and did (John 21:25). Some New Testament interpreters have suggested that Matthew 5–7 is a collection of teachings from Jesus' Galilean ministry, which occurred over a period of many months. I would prefer as an interpreter of the text to allow these chapters of Matthew to stand, as they do in his Gospel, without such an elaborate explanation. But it does seem reasonable that Matthew has condensed Jesus' teachings from this lakeside meeting so that in the Sermon on the Mount we read only the major epigrams and conclusions of perhaps hours of teaching.

If this is so, let me invite you to wonder about the listeners' reactions and questions. If there were moments when the disciples were invited to ask questions, what might they have asked? Are there places in the sermon where it seems that Jesus is aware of what is on their minds and then answers these concerns? And what about you in the twentieth century: What questions do you have about the amazing teachings of this sermon? What parts of the sermon stir you to have questions, and what are those questions?

What are you going to do with these three chapters of Matthew? Can the words of Jesus possibly apply to moderns like ourselves who live in the complicated social, racial, and national communities of the twentieth century? Let me invite you into the words of Jesus. I believe that the best way to read this remarkable sermon is to try to dialogue with the teacher at all of the radical edges in it—to raise our own questions each step of the way and then to experience the surprises that come through as the sermon takes on its whole form and message. The whole sermon is hardly mild; there is a good wildness in the sermon and yet at the same time the teacher is friendly toward those who

---

* Examples of this compression are the Book of Acts records of the sermons of Peter and Paul (Acts 2, 17).

are undone by the intensity of the message's demands. Read Jesus' words with your heart as well as your mind, with your will for the present and future as much as with your experience of the past.

It is my conclusion as a textual and theological interpreter that the soundest interpretive model for the reader of this sermon is that approach which treats these three chapters of Matthew's Gospel as a whole fabric. The sermon is placed by Matthew within the Galilean ministry of Jesus and portrayed as an incident in that ministry.

No part of the New Testament has received the same amount of scholarly attention as have the three chapters we call the Sermon on the Mount. This close attention began very early in the Christian church. The church fathers, from the early second-century *Didache* to Chrysostom, had more specifically to say about this special passage than any other part of the New Testament. Since that time, most of the giants of Christian theology have written commentaries on it. Augustine, Aquinas, Calvin, Luther, Bonhoeffer—all wrote their interpretations. An excellent survey of the history of interpretation of the Sermon on the Mount by its many interpreters and commentators is presented in Robert A. Guelich's *The Sermon on the Mount.*

A major question among many interpreters has to do with source theory for the Sermon on the Mount material. The most common hypothesis argues that Matthew has drawn most of the teaching material from source "Q," and that Luke did the same for his presentation of the Sermon on the Plain (Luke 6:20–49). But this elaborate search for the source Q threads within Matthew 5–7 is a basically artificial hypothesis with no concrete documentation or manuscript evidence to sustain it.* It seems more probable to me that what we find in the sermon is an example of

---

* The existence of "Q" is not in my view as useful an interpretive hypothesis as the more obvious conclusion that the Synoptic writers quote from each other: Matthew first, then Mark, who has the benefit of Matthew's text. Finally, Luke has before him both the texts of Matthew and Mark.

a message Jesus may have often spoken. It is brief; it has the sound of the kind of wisdom teaching found in Proverbs, which would be epigrammatic in nature and could be followed by dialogue as listeners raised questions of the teacher. Matthew presents the sermon as a simple whole with the strong beginning of proverb-like poetry and the strong close of the parable on house-building in the face of storms. It seems to me that very impressive literary evidence is needed to shift our interpretative stance away from this most obvious direction toward which Matthew the writer leads his readers. The fact is that when the document we call the Sermon on the Mount is treated as a collection of sayings ("merely a collection of unrelated sayings of diverse origins, a patchwork . . ."), the result is that the total effect of the teaching is sharply diminished because we as readers then lose the connectedness of the sermon which is what gives it force and power.

I will endeavor to show in this commentary that there is indeed that very meaningful and essential connectedness within the sermon so that the crises posed in one part of the sermon work toward a powerful question or resolution in another part of the text. W. D. Davies's comments have no foundation in the literary examination of the text itself because there is a literary unity in the material. This causes the sermon to make good literary sense. And this unity grants it its remarkable persuasiveness and universal appeal as well as its intense theological hitting force.

But finally we must ask the fundamental interpretative question: What is the meaning of this sermon for us today?

Is the sermon basically good advice about the way of righteousness? Was Leo Tolstoy correct in his admiration of this sermon? "Let men only do this, and we should have the kingdom of God on earth." Or should we accept Albert Schweitzer's pessimistic viewpoint about it? He saw this sermon as "an emergency ethic for his disciples' use during the brief interval between his preaching and the cataclysmic coming of his kingdom." Therefore, in Schweitzer's view, this teaching is inferior and in the end tragic since for

Schweitzer, the Teacher of the ethic failed to establish his kingdom on earth.

Some interpreters have treated the sermon as an "Ethic of Attitude." Martin Dibelius takes this view, but the result is a wistfulness in his teaching about the sermon. At each decisive point the Lion in the sermon is caged and tamed by the "Ethic of Attitude" approach. Professor Dibelius in his lectures on the Sermon on the Mount in 1939 seems to call into question his own earlier handling of the text where he concludes with a brilliant remark: "A vague Christian idealism is insufficient as a basis for the witness we must bear. We must trace our convictions back to the Bible, the only common source of our faith." [2] But the "Ethic of Attitude" is precisely the vague Christian idealism Dr. Dibelius rejects.

A fourth view is what A. M. Hunter calls the theological view. "The purpose of the sermon is to bring home to us the awful fact that we are sinners, and so prepare us for Christ's proper work. . . ." Dr. Hunter is on target with this comment; he has recognized the profoundly Messianic nature of our Lord's sermon which properly includes the ethics and the eschatological messianic purpose of the words of Jesus.

Another view sees this sermon primarily as a portrayal of the fulfillment of the future coming kingdom of God. This view is held by dispensational teachers. "The study of the sermon on the mount yields its treasures to those who analyze each text determining its general meaning, its present application, and its relation to the future kingdom program." [3]

There are elements of truth in each view. There is teaching and "advice" in this sermon; there is immediacy and urgency, as Schweitzer saw, but not the urgency of a failed kingdom, because the Lord of the sermon also became in history the Lord of the victory over death. There is a whole new attitude and perspective toward life in the sermon; the kingdom to come is breaking in with this sermon because of the Living King who is present in it.

THE
ENORMOUS
EXCEPTION

1
THE ROAD

Blessed are the poor in spirit, for theirs is the kingdom of heaven.

Blessed are those who mourn, for they shall be comforted.

Blessed are the meek, for they shall inherit the earth.

Blessed are those who hunger and thirst for righteousness, for they shall be satisfied.

Blessed are the merciful, for they shall obtain mercy.

Blessed are the pure in heart, for they shall see God.

Blessed are the peacemakers, for they shall be called sons of God.

Blessed are those who are persecuted for righteousness' sake, for theirs is the kingdom of heaven.

Blessed are you when men revile you and persecute you and utter all kinds of evil against you falsely on my account. Rejoice and be glad, for your reward is great in heaven, for so men persecuted the prophets who were before you.

(Matt. 5:3–12)

The one word Jesus uses nine times in the beginning of the sermon is translated in most English Bibles "blessed." The word in the Greek language means happy. Jesus might have given this sermon in Hebrew or in Galilean Aramaic (the local northern dialect of first-century Palestine). Or he might have taught in Greek, since most people in the Mediterranean world could speak and understand Greek. But whatever language he used, one fact is clear; the language that underpins his thinking is Hebrew.

"Jesus lived in the Old Testament. His sayings are incomprehensible unless we realize this," says Joachim Jeremias. The Hebrew word for *blessed* or *happy* is very interesting, and our understanding of this Old Testament word will help us appreciate what it means in the Beatitudes, since Hebrew meanings are behind the Greek vocabulary word choices in the sermon.

The Hebrew word for "blessed" is *ashr*. Proverbs 3:13, 17 says, "Blessed is the man who finds wisdom. . . . Her ways are pleasant ways, and all her paths are peace." *Ashr* in Proverbs means to find the right path. If you are surrounded by many confusing ways and find the right way to go, then you are happy. This Old Testament idea of happiness has to do with orientation, perspective, the discovery of what is meaningful in the midst of shallow, superficial options.

Jesus gives nine proverbs on the way to happiness to draw us into the most electrifying sermon ever preached. This ninefold way of (*ashr*) happiness can be divided into three parts.

The first four beatitudes are reflective, intensely personal portrayals, which might be called the inner pathway:

1. Happy are the poor in *spirit,* that is, those who know they are poor.

2. Happy are those who *mourn,* those who feel deeply the sense of loss and the pain that goes with it.

3. Happy are the *meek,* or those who have a sane evaluation of themselves.

4. Happy are those who *hunger* and *thirst* for *righteousness,* those who have moved beyond the various false options of this generation and have decided to seek God's truth and character.

The second part tells of three important life-style ingredients. Jesus teaches three specific marks of the way of happiness in these beatitudes:

5. Happy are the *merciful,* those who really love people, not in a theoretical sense, but in a concrete way.

6. Happy are the *pure in heart,* those who have simplified and uncluttered their affections, having chosen to obey the righteous will of God.

7. Happy are the *peacemakers,* that is, those who share the health and wholeness of peace with the people around them.

The third part concludes with two hard and terrifying beatitudes united in poetic parallelism.

8. Happy are those who are *persecuted* because of righteousness.

9. Happy are those who are *persecuted* on Christ's account.

Jesus surprises us by using one of the harshest words in the Greek language, "persecute," which means "to run after, to pursue." He teaches that it is possible to find the right pathway even in the midst of a less-than-ideal setting; a Christian can survive within a hostile environment. Notice also the vital theological fact that Jesus has united *righteousness* with his own *personal lordship:* "persecuted because of righteousness . . . because of me."

When we understand the rich meanings of the Old Testament background for the word *blessed,* we can make the deepest sort of sense of the Beatitudes. Jesus has not only drawn together a poetic tour de force, but there is also something profoundly realistic and significant in each of the apparently strange uses of the word *happy.* It seems strange by any ordinary standard to say that one who is profoundly thirsty, or who mourns, or who is persecuted should be happy! But Jesus is telling us that we are on the right path when we know of our own hunger, when we are sensitive to sorrow, and when our way of truth is under attack. In fact, Jesus teaches that in the deepest sense the nature of happiness is to be on that very pathway.

Have you ever experienced a perilous moment in your own life when you felt particularly exposed to dangers, when you were most vulnerable, and yet you knew inside at a very deep personal level that you were in the right place at the right time? Perhaps at just such a moment you realized you were on the pathway where Jesus Christ was leading you. It may have seemed odd to others, but at that very moment in spite of its gravity it was for you a joyous moment too. You experienced in that mixture of gravity and joy the very heart of the meaning of the Beatitudes of Jesus. You experienced a happiness not founded upon happenings or circumstances but upon a joy rooted in the deeper source of God's grace. When it struck you that this was true, you surprised yourself and others around you by the shock of recognition that this very place, hard and difficult as it was, nevertheless was the place where you wanted to be. You were in that deepest of all ways, happy!

Do you remember Frodo and Sam Gangi on the dark pathways beneath the ominous tower in J. R. R. Tolkien's *The Two Towers?* Do you remember that scene when they begin to wonder about the meaning of everything they are now experiencing on their journey? They wonder if future generations might remember their adventures which now are dangerously threatening and frightful. They wonder about some future moment when the friendship experiences of the two travelers will become more important than the dangers, and when their mission for good has won out against the devastating power of evil. Listen to the way Tolkien portrays that scene.

Frodo and his loyal friend Sam Gangi begin to imagine

together about the stories that will someday be told about their dangerous mission. Sam Gangi speaks:

"Still, I wonder if we shall ever be put into songs or tales. We're in one, of course; but I mean: put into words, you know, told by the fireside, or read out of a great big book with red and black letters, years and years afterwards. And people will say: 'Let's hear about Frodo and the ring!' And they'll say: 'Yes, that's one of my favourite stories. Frodo was very brave, wasn't he, dad?' 'Yes, my boy, the famousest of the hobbits, and that's saying a lot.' "

"It's saying a lot too much," said Frodo, and he laughed, a long clear laugh from his heart. Such a sound had not been heard in those places since Sauron came to Middle-earth. . . . he laughed again. "Why, Sam," he said, "to hear you somehow makes me as merry as if the story was already written. But you've left out one of the chief characters: Samwise the stouthearted." [1]

Frodo and Sam have experienced the breakthrough of the word *blessed*. Let evil beware of such laughter, of such happiness. It is a sign of the greater power of good overcoming the power of evil. Suddenly it dawns upon us that the Tower of Mordor is not as awesome as we thought. The laughter of the two pilgrims springs from their sudden awareness of the fact that they have been blessed. They are where they are supposed to be! They are on the right road.

A Frontal Challenge

Let me put this in another way. The only way the Beatitudes of Jesus make sense is if Jesus Christ himself, the one who speaks them, is strong enough to make them really true. We are able to endure persecution and actually to believe we are on the right path if our companion in the middle of that persecution is the living Lord. These Beatitudes are the words of authority; they boldly challenge every way of looking at life that people ordinarily hold. Chesterton puts it this way:

The statement that the meek shall inherit the earth is very far from being a meek statement. The blessing upon the meek would seem to be a very violent statement, in the sense of doing violence to reason and probability. Most critics who are offended at things Jesus says are offended precisely because Jesus does not utter safe platitudes.[2]

The one thing we must see is that the Beatitudes, by which Jesus begins this sermon, are *not* a mild and sentimental collection of platitudes. They are a frontal challenge to almost everything we assume about "the way it is" in the world. The only way they make sense is if Jesus Christ himself is able to sustain the blessings he pronounces. When that fact becomes our fact, and when we become convinced that Jesus Christ has the authority to support his promises, then the word *blessed* not only invites us to find the right path but also to welcome the path we find.

We now have the biblical doctrine of success. Success is not measured in possessions or by the state of our health. Success means to be where I am supposed to be—the right place at the right time and for the right reason—because of the purpose for my life that has its origins in God's love and faithfulness. If I am on the right road then I am successful in this radical rearrangement of our ordinary value systems. Success for those who believe this amazing Sermon on the Mount is a word about relationship with the Shepherd-Lord of the pathway and about our journey upon that pathway.

Additional Notes

I have pointed up the significance of the ninefold use of the word *bless* in the opening of Jesus' sermon. It is my contention that the Hebrew understanding of bless as seen in the word *ashr* is the most valuable clue to Jesus' intention in his repetitive use of the word. I believe his intention is in the sense of *ashr* whether he taught the sermon in Greek, Hebrew or Aramaic. The fact is clearly demonstrated in New Testament studies that Jesus was thinking in Jewish terms though he was capable of speaking in koine Greek (first-century popular Greek), as were most first-century Jews. The Greek word *makarios* is used in the Greek text for "happy"; throughout its classical Greek usage "from Aristotle onward it is used to describe the social stratum of the wealthy who in virtue of their riches are above normal cares and worries of lesser folk." [3] But the context makes it clear that Jesus does not have Aristotle's "happy" in mind when he uses this word; he is thinking of the blessing of Psalm 1 with its earthy and richly colored roadway meanings. The proof of this is that the opening blessing is spoken for the poor. I must offer at this point a word of caution on word studies. They are valuable only if they are made in careful connection with the literary contextual whole of the sentence in which they appear. David Hill, in *Greek Words and Hebrew Meanings,* explains the value of word studies very well when he says, "Every word is a semantic marker for a field of meaning, a pointer to what Barr calls 'a wide area of recognized thought.'" James Barr in his significant study points up, "It is the sentence . . . which is the linguistic bearer of the usual theological statement and not the word. . . ." [4] Therefore we who study New Testament texts should carefully pursue individual word studies, but we must keep in perspective the meanings of the word as it appears in its sentence.

2
SALT AND LIGHT

You are the salt of the earth; but if salt has lost its taste, how shall its saltness be restored? It is no longer good for anything except to be thrown out and trodden under foot by men.

You are the light of the world. A city set on a hill cannot be hid. Nor do men light a lamp and put it under a bushel, but on a stand, and it gives light to all in the house. Let your light so shine before men, that they may see your good works and give glory to your Father who is in heaven.

(Matt. 5:13–16)

Following the nine great sentences, Jesus presents his disciples with two fascinating images: 1) You are the *salt* of the earth. 2) You are the *light* of the world.

Within these sentences lies an obvious and exciting contrast. The one is hidden; the other is visible. Salt cannot easily be seen when it is added to food, but its preservative power is tasted, and its good effect is experienced. When fish is salted, it does not spoil but remains nutritious and edible for many days. Salt is essential not only as a pleasant ingredient in the human diet but also for the very survival of human health.

But salt is not so much a taste as it is a flavorful preservative. It is this preservative effect that in fact makes it dangerous if we think of it as a spice or flavor. A little salt goes a long way; if misused it will become a dangerous hardener of blood vessels and arteries. I believe it is this basic preserving nature of salt that Jesus intends in this figure more than the flavorful side effect it has on French fries.

Every listener in the first-century Mediterranean world would be able to appreciate the importance of this salt image. The value of salt is tested not by the way it appears but by what happens as a result of its use. It has no value apart from its preserving and mineral-nourishing benefits. If it were to lose its purity as salt because of contamination by other chemicals, it would not only fall short of its purpose but would become a threat to food and health. Salt has therefore this hiddenness about it, and later in the Sermon on the Mount Jesus will teach in specific detail about the value and meaning of hiddenness.

What Shall Be Done With Nonsalty Salt?

Jesus here both honors and warns his followers by the reference to salt. "You are the salt. . . . but if the salt loses. . . ." Jesus warns us not to lose God's intended purpose for our lives. We have been destined to be like salt, and that divine intention is a very serious matter. If we were to lose that intended purpose we would be confronted then by the obvious and hard question of Jesus: What shall be done with nonsalty salt?

But if there is a warning in this teaching, there is also a promise. "You *are* the salt. . . ." Jesus has affirmed to his disciples what his will is for their lives. It is his will that his disciples be saltlike. It is his intention to involve his disciples in his own preservation-and-health ministry in the world. We, as disciples of Jesus Christ, are to share in the great salty purposes he has for the world.

The same mixture of challenge and promise is present in the image of *light*. Light has to do with finding our way, as a hiker who looks for some fixed point in order to know where the trail leads. Jesus commands his disciples to let light shine so that the journeyers alongside our lives may find the pathway of God's will.

What is the theological and discipleship significance of these verses for us today?

They give us a vivid portrait of the will of God for human life. God wants a healthy created order to survive the spoiling assaults against it, and God wants that created order to find its true Center, the way of light.

What is the meaning of that way of salt and light? We must develop our answer on the basis of the nine Beatitudes. We will be given other clues as we study the remaining teachings of the Sermon on the Mount, but at this point in the sermon that Jesus is preaching our primary clues to his meanings come from the roadway language of the Beatitudes.

As we read this "salt-and-light" passage and other teachings of Christ, we may be troubled that Jesus should include warnings along with promises. We may think he has taken away the joy of the promises by the very fact of the warnings. His teaching puts a continuous challenge to us, even over against us. We see later in the Gospels this same mixture as, for example, in the Caesarea Philippi incident: "For whoever would save his life will lose it, and whoever loses his life for my sake and for the gospel's will save it" (Mark

8:35). We see it in his words to the church at Ephesus in Revelation 2:5: ". . . do the works you did at first. If not, I will come to you and remove your lampstand from its place, unless you repent."

Promise and Warning

But in the midst of promises and warnings, one fact is clear: the will of God is a serious matter and it is not to be taken lightly. His intention for our lives is not a marginal note, a luxury to be added to our lives as an enrichment. Jesus portrays his purpose for life as *essential* and *crucial* to the very survival of the created order. If we felt our need of Jesus Christ before these words, we now feel that need even more. His words in the nine Beatitudes have honored us, and now our discovery of how important his intention is for us has sobered us. However, without a greater source of strength and aid than what we know in ourselves, the prospects are discouraging.

But what a remarkable combination of promise and warning! It is something like the pregame speech a football coach might give to his starting players. "Each of you has been honored by my choice as your coach that makes you a member of the starting lineup. However, if you linemen miss your blocks and if you wide receivers drop the ball I don't think I have to remind you of what will happen. I will pull you out of the game." We live with this mixture of promise and demand in every important endeavor because something basic about that twofold mixture is etched into the building blocks of every great endeavor. Freedom and responsibility, giftedness and obligation always sooner or later stand up alongside each other. Jesus agrees with this fundamental principle, but the difference has to do with both the power of the giftedness and the importance of the great endeavor. Jesus is describing the very survival of the earth that is now mysteriously related to the salt-and-light description he has assigned to his disciples. The game is more vital than any sporting event we know of and the power that Jesus grants to his team goes beyond any of the powers of which this earth is capable. Perhaps now we can understand why the Lord of the Sermon on the Mount has added solemn warnings to the promises.

Our hope of experiencing the promise lies in the fact that it is Jesus Christ who has spoken. He is the source of both true light and true saltiness. The authority of the disciples is, therefore, derivative, not original. The task Jesus gives to his disciples does not mean that his disciples become saviors or sustainers of the earth in the place of Jesus Christ. Jesus remains the Lord, and the Savior, and yet in the mystery of his prior authority. Jesus Christ draws his disciples into the task that he, the Savior-Lord, is about. That "drawing-in" of our lives into the purpose of Christ's ministry is what these two remarkable promises are about.

The important discipleship question the Christian must ask of these words of Jesus is: How do I live out this form of discipleship in a practical way, so that the hidden saltiness and the visible light are both fulfilled?

If we are salt, what are we to preserve?

I believe Jesus is here signaling his high valuation of human life. As Paul's presence in the Roman prison ship became for the sailors and others on board a preserving fact (see Acts 27, 28), so our presence in the history of real people in real places is mysteriously and powerfully a preservative reality. What God preserves by and through our ministries in obedience to Jesus Christ is what he chooses to preserve, but the amazing fact is that we play a part in that holy decision of God to sustain the created order.

The very presence of a Christian who shares the love of Jesus Christ has a humanizing effect upon the concrete human situations that he or she is set into, and by the impact of that lived-out discipleship the people around that person benefit from the saltiness and the light. What has been preserved is the worth of persons who are seen now in the light of God's will. The "city set on a hill" shows a new goal for life that originates from God's love, God's character.

I remember a premedicine undergraduate at University

of California Berkeley who became a Christian after a long journey through doubts and questions. I asked him what were some of the key factors that helped to tip the scales in favor of Jesus Christ for him in that spiritual journey and he told me of a bout with the flu that had hit him very hard during the previous school term, forcing him to miss ten days of school. During that critical absence from his organic chemistry class a classmate who happened to be a Christian carefully collected all assignments and work for him in the chemistry class and then took the time away from his own studies to help him catch up to the rest of the class. The student said to me, "You know that this just isn't done and I probably wouldn't have done it, but he gave that help to me without any fanfare or complaints. I wanted to know what made this friend of mine act the way he did; I found myself asking him if I could go to church with him." God had used a salt-and-light Christian to tip the scales in the life of this student toward the Lord who cares about students who want to learn organic chemistry and eventually become doctors. His friend was toward him a preservative influence and an encouragement so that in that practical and what might appear quite small series of events his friend and fellow student had been able to find the way of an even more profound preservation of life. I think the best tribute I ever heard concerning a Christian was the tribute spoken of this student. "I felt more alive when I was around this friend." It is this life that the disciples felt when they were near Jesus and it is what the world still feels when its people are near to those who know Jesus.

Aleksandr Solzhenitsyn's *One Day in the Life of Ivan Denisovich* portrays this reality in the character of the young prisoner Alyoska "reading his Gospels with his face toward the lightbulb." Alyoska has a profoundly humanizing effect upon the cynical and yet searching Ivan. The meaning of Ivan's life has been deepened and preserved by his encounter with his young Christian friend. Though Ivan gives no outward sign of following the pathway to which Alyoska points, nevertheless the way has been illuminated to him. He has experienced from a fellow prisoner the salt and light of that One who is greater than the prisoners in a human and degraded world, and now his own life is more significant; it has been preserved by the God who loves him through Alyoska as Alyoska tries his best to share his hope with Ivan at the close of a work day. Ivan was always loved by God, and Jesus Christ has already won the victory in his behalf over sin and death and the devil. The Christian Alyoska has made that holy decision of God in Jesus Christ physically present alongside Ivan, just as Paul did in his witness toward the crew and passengers of a slave ship in the storm off Malta.

This does not mean that one disciple who has faith in Christ is a stand-in for those around, so that as long as one person believes, all the others are covered by his or her faith. No, our freedom and responsibility are not compromised in such a fashion. Ivan must still make up his own mind about the good promises of the gospel. Nevertheless, there is a mystery here—Ivan has been blessed by knowing Alyoska. And so will others who are touched by your salt and light.

Additional Notes

"If the salt loses its saltness"—the Greek verb used in this text is the unusual word *moranthe* which could be best translated "low grade." Understanding the word in that sense, I have interpreted Jesus' intention in the analogy to be "contaminated salt." Albright notes that in the Middle East at that time there was the danger of salts becoming contaminated by such impurities as gypsum, natron, and sodium sulphate.[1]

"Light." I believe Jesus has in mind the *light* in the Old Testament sense of Psalm 119:105, "Thy word is a lamp to my feet and a light to my path." It is this same sense of the word that is intended in the words of Jesus as recorded in the Gospel of John (8:12)—"I am the light of the world; he who follows me will not walk in darkness, . . ."

The interpreters who see the "light" references in the New Testament as examples of Gnostic influences upon New Testament writers have ignored the profoundly Jewish nature of the references. Rudolph Bultmann treats the opening prologue in John's Gospel (1:1–18) as if it were a Stoic hymn, but in my view that is just what the opening song in John's Gospel is not! It is a Jewish song that honors the God of creation who speaks for himself in flesh and brings light into darkness. The hymn sounds more like Psalm 119 than it does the Stoic hymns of Greek mythology. These "light" references as in the Sermon on the Mount are decidedly not "Gnostic motifs" as Bultmann suggests in his *Theology of the New Testament*. Jesus is not offering "light" to his disciples in the Sermon on the Mount as an escape from the real world. Rather, Jesus uses this image of light as a part of his mandate to the disciples to stay creatively related to the roadway; it is light for the pathway just as the Torah is light for the pathway. Instead of light as an image of escape, it becomes the enablement for involvement. That is precisely the point.

3
LORD OF THE LAW

Think not that I have come to abolish the law and the prophets; I have come not to abolish them but to fulfil them. For truly, I say to you, till heaven and earth pass away, not an iota, not a dot, will pass from the law until all is accomplished. Whoever then relaxes one of the least of these commandments and teaches men so, shall be called least in the kingdom of heaven; but he who does them and teaches them shall be called great in the kingdom of heaven. For I tell you, unless your righteousness exceeds that of the scribes and Pharisees, you will never enter the kingdom of heaven.

(Matt. 5:17–20)

Jesus now takes into his hands the Jewish people's whole experience and memory of the past. No part of that tradition is more vital to the Jews than the Law of God as given to Moses. The Torah is even more than that; it is the consensus of the people's life together. Even though Israel did not obey the Law faithfully there nevertheless is a nonnegotiable ethos, an agreement, that surrounds the Torah. This is represented by the way the scrolls of the Torah are presented and cared for by the synagogue and in the way the copiers were required to exactly preserve even the distinctive spacing and indentation calibrations of the Law as a document.

At this point Jesus could conceivably move in several directions in his sermon.

Three Options

He could *reject* everything in the people's past: their traditions and their Law. Some few listeners might have welcomed just that sort of scorched-earth approach. After all, even with the possession of the Law of Moses and the traditions that grew out of the Law, as a people they were apparently little better off under Roman oppression than during the time more than twelve hundred years earlier in the wilderness when they first received the Torah. When some people feel that kind of social and political helplessness, they often welcome prophets who throw out the past with its apparent impotence, and offer what appears to be a totally new option. Dietrich Bonhoeffer described this mood and desire in his *Letters and Papers from Prison* as those who want a "fruitful radicalism in the place of a barren mediocrity." [1] Could it not have been argued that the Law of Mount Sinai had failed?

Another group who might have welcomed the discarding of the Law were those who felt personally trapped and demoralized by it. The Law represented condemnation to them because they felt its weight upon their shoulders, and if Jesus were to cancel it, he would probably have had their support. If we feel condemned by the Law because of certain of our sins we might welcome the elimination of the document that makes us feel guilty.

Jesus could also take the opposite approach; he could simply and plainly *restate* the Law as the common tradition of the people. He might return strictly to the texts of the Pentateuch, or he might include the broader way of the Pharisees, whose later traditions of interpretation had been refined since the time of the Maccabean Revolt (about 160 B.C.). If Jesus were to favor the more limited way, he would have the support of the Sadducee party; if he were to favor the broader restatement, he would have the support of the Pharisee party.

The Great Arc of the Law

Jesus chooses a third way, and risks the disappointment of all the special interest groups now waiting to hear his teaching. He takes hold of the Law and the traditions that surround the Ten Commandments as if they were an unfinished portrait; he now draws together the separate parts of the Law toward the completion of their original intention. Think of it this way; Jesus treats the Law as if it were a great arc. He now extends the line of the arc around to its fulfillment, the circle for which it was originally designed.

Jesus completes the circle, and that is the meaning of the word that he uses to describe his purpose: *fulfill.* Fulfill

means literally to "fill up or complete." C. S. Lewis explains this by asking us to think of our whole experience of tradition and law and life itself as an unfinished symphony or novel. Now, in the breakthrough of the grand miracle of Jesus Christ, there is introduced the main theme of the symphony or novel. The result of this discovery is that "at every fresh hearing of the music, or every fresh reading of the book, we should find it settling down, making itself more at home, and eliciting significance from all sorts of details in the whole work which we had hitherto neglected." [2] Jesus completes the circle; he integrates the novel; the symphony is finally completed.

The claims Jesus Christ makes in these opening words of the Sermon on the Mount are remarkable for their boldness. His words imply that he is the one who fulfills the very intent of the Law itself, because as Jesus dares to take the Law into his hands, he has dared to interpret its central purpose.

Jesus not only claims his authority with regard to the Law; he also claims to fulfill the expectations of the prophets. "Law and Prophets" is the phrase a first-century Jew would use to describe the essence of the Old Testament message. Therefore we may conclude that Jesus by these words lays hold not only of the Ten Commandments, or even the codes of the Pentateuch, or beyond that to their enlargement in Pharisaic tradition. But his claims include the whole Old Testament expectation, teaching, and history. Jesus Christ is the rightful fulfillment of it all! We are standing at the source and the completion of the whole of the promises, warnings, and teachings.

Three Threads

We are now at the theological center of the Sermon on the Mount. The sermon's credibility will depend upon the character of this Jesus who makes such claims, because he has so boldly gathered to himself all of the great themes of Old Testament expectation. Theologically, what has happened is that the Abrahamic, Mosaic, and Davidic threads of Old Testament history and expectation have now converged in the Lord of the sermon.

The Old Testament expectations might be described as three great yearnings of God's people which are focused in Old Testament history in the journey experiences of three outstanding figures of holy history:

Abrahamic Thread
————————————————————————————————————→
    The yearning for identity
Mosaic Thread
————————————————————————————————————→
    The yearning for deliverance
Davidic Thread
————————————————————————————————————→
    The yearning for the kingdom

These three threads were drawn together first by the psalmists and prophets, who agonized over the meanings of identity, Exodus (salvation from outward oppression), and Law (salvation from inner oppression). Together with the joyous yearning for kingdom in the Davidic thread these yearnings make up the essential ingredients of the character of the Israelite people. Though all such models are oversimplified, the model of the three threads may be helpful in making sense of what we find in Old Testament history and song.

The Jewish feasts and religious practices expressed in graphic and ceremonial ways these yearnings of sacred Scripture. For example, circumcision was the sign of the identity thread; it reminded Israel that they were Abraham's people and inheritors of Abraham's promise. The feasts were vivid reminders of the Exodus redemption (Passover), the giving of the Law (Feast of Pentecost), and the protection by God through forty years in the wilderness (Feast of Tabernacles). The Feast of Dedication, though commemorating the heroic victory of Judas Maccabaeus, was at heart very

Davidic and kingdom-oriented. In other words, the people's tradition continually reminded them of who they were, from what they had escaped, and the goal toward which their destiny lay.

In a profound sense, the inner meanings of these threads are also present in the yearnings of all people, and not only the people of the Old Testament, though they are expressed by different histories and by different signs.[3]

Now we come to the radical center of the Sermon on the Mount. Jesus Christ makes the claim that these profound streams of holy history properly and meaningfully converge in himself. This is the only way in which the bold word "fulfill" can be understood. It is Jesus of Nazareth who really completes our yearning for identity, so that we know who we are and to what end that ancient promise to Abraham was made, " 'by you all the families of the earth shall bless themselves.' " It is Jesus who fulfills the righteous will of God shown at Mount Sinai and he is able to incarnate in himself the Way (Torah) for which the Law was given in the first place. Jesus Christ is also David's King, the one whom the wise men sought on the first Christmas. He is the only one good enough to resolve David's sin and great enough to fulfill David's dream.

Jesus—the Law's Fulfillment

The theological significance of this fulfillment is very far reaching, as we shall see in the remainder of the Sermon on the Mount. It means that all Old Testament teaching needs to be interpreted in the context of its fulfillment in the gospel. Jesus at this point in the sermon makes a promise to his listeners in this regard (v. 18): He promises that as the Old Testament Law and Prophets are read through the lens of their fulfillment in the preacher of the sermon they will not be sabotaged or distorted by this fulfillment lens. Rather, their original design will become all the clearer.

Because Jesus Christ is the fulfillment of these yearnings he concludes this part of his teaching with another warning

(v. 19). He cautions that the Law and the Prophets are not to be diminished or disregarded by his followers; in fact, his words will intensify, not lessen, the demand of the holy Law of God. The Law and the Prophets are a vital part of the whole and, therefore, they stand as signs that point toward this fulfillment in God's Messiah. Put another way, they are a true and faithful, though incomplete, arc of the circle that now is completed in its Lord.

For those of us who read this sermon today we may wonder about the contemporary significance of this fulfillment theology for our lives and discipleship. The first and most obvious discovery we make from these words of Jesus is that the ancient Law which is so important to the life of the Old Testament people is also of great importance for our life as Christians today. Because of Jesus' words we who trust in his Lordship over all of life including the Law must now trust in the Law which has its completion in the Lord we trust.

There is something else, however, that these words of Jesus bring into clear focus for us. The great threads of yearning and expectation that are gathered together in a phrase like "the law and the prophets" have signaled to us the reality of our own complicated yearnings and hopes. Most of us have not actually journeyed with Israel in the story of its profound hopes and longings for Messiah, but we have had our own journeys with different motifs and different symbols. We may not have a Moses in our own story but we do have "exodus" and "deliverance" experiences and hopes for deliverance in our memory of the past. We know of our own good catastrophes when at a dark moment help came by surprise. We have our own stories about such moments of help and from those stories we in our own way yearn for redemption, for freedom; we hope for the resolution of deeply felt awkwardness and alienation. We may not know of Moses and his tribe of oppressed Jews in Egypt, but we know of oppression in our own terms and in the places where we live our lives. All this means that the Mosaic yearning for deliverance is a very deeply-felt spiritual and consciousness thread in every human being that cries out for resolution. Our movies, our novels, our art, and our music tell in different ways the profound search for freedom from despair and meaninglessness. The words we use are not religious words and that proves the universality of the yearning all the more.

It is also true that the identity thread of Israel with its rich Abrahamic heritage and its ceremony of circumcision of the male on the eighth day of his life may not represent our own sense of who we are, but the search for identity and belongingness is a profoundly felt one in every human being. "Who am I?" is as old a question as "who are you?"; they go together. These identity yearnings for a father like Abraham have their equivalents in every human story of culture and tribe.

The Davidic thread is the search for kingdom, for success, for happiness and it also is a universal quest. It was Blaise Pascal who wrote in his *Pensées,* "Man wants to be happy, only wants to be happy, and cannot help wanting to be happy." And again: "The Stoics say: 'Withdraw into yourself, that is where you will find peace,' and that is not true. Others say: 'Go outside. Look for happiness in some diversion,' and that is not true; we may fall sick. Happiness is neither outside nor inside us; it is in God, both outside and inside us." [4]

In these two quotations the three threads converge. Our yearning for kingdom is spoiled by our confusion about who we are, the identity crisis, and until we are delivered from that confusion we will never be able to experience fulfillment. We can now appreciate St. Paul's sermon on Mars Hill to the philosophers of Athens. He proclaimed to them that Jesus Christ is the fulfillment of the ancient search of the philosophers of Greece just as he is the fulfillment of Israel's quest for a king like David, a father like Abraham, and a redeemer like Moses. Israel looked for the way of this righteousness—Greece looked for the reason of this righteousness. Jesus Christ has completed the arc of both circles.

Additional Notes

Torah, the Hebrew word for Law, is used two hundred twenty-one times in the Old Testament. The word comes from the root *yara,* which means *way,* and therefore *Torah* means literally and concretely "the way found." (See the extensive discussion of Torah in the author's book *Old Law New Life,* The Ten Commandments and New Testament Faith, published by Abingdon in 1984.) The Law for Israel is "a statement of community ethos, a definitional statement of the character of the community which is given and is not negotiable among the new generation." [5]

The concrete and historically definite nature of discipleship is preserved by Jesus. He stands clearly in the same tradition as the Law and Prophets of the Old Testament. The revelation of God's Torah stands as a concrete reality alongside our lives, and Jesus preserves that call of the Law to all who would belong to the way of righteousness. He does not spiritualize the Law; therefore the integrity of the Law and its historical significance is heightened by Jesus and not diminished. ". . . God did enter a covenant with a historical people at a particular time and place . . . this biblical witness remains a warning against spiritualizing the covenant and the demands of the Law. . . . The externality of God's revelation at Sinai guards the church from encapsulating God within the good intentions of the religious conscience." [6]

4
PEOPLE PROTECTION

You have heard that it was said to the men of old, "You shall not kill; and whoever kills shall be liable to judgment." But I say to you that every one who is angry with his brother shall be liable to judgment; whoever insults his brother shall be liable to the council, and whoever says, "You fool!" shall be liable to the hell of fire. So if you are offering your gift at the altar, and there remember that your brother has something against you, leave your gift there before the altar and go; first be reconciled to your brother, and then come and offer your gift. Make friends quickly with your accuser, while you are going with him to court, lest your accuser hand you over to the judge, and the judge to the guard, and you be put in prison; truly, I say to you, you will never get out till you have paid the last penny.

You have heard that it was said, "You shall not commit adultery." But I say to you that every one who looks at a woman lustfully has already committed adultery with her in his heart. If your right eye causes you to sin, pluck it out and throw it away; it is better that you lose one of your members than that your whole body be thrown into hell. And if your right hand causes you to sin, cut it off and throw it away; it is better that you lose one of your members than that your whole body go into hell.

It was also said, "Whoever divorces his wife, let him give her a certificate of divorce." But I say to you that every one who divorces his wife, except on the ground of unchastity, makes her an adulteress; and whoever marries a divorced woman commits adultery.

Again you have heard that it was said to the men of old, "You shall not swear falsely, but shall perform to the Lord what you have sworn." But I say to you, Do not swear at all, either by heaven, for it is the throne of God, or by the earth, for it is his footstool, or by Jerusalem, for it is the city of the great King. And do not swear by your head, for you cannot make one hair white or black. Let what you say be simply "Yes" or "No"; anything more than this comes from evil.

(Matt. 5:21–37)

Let us watch how Jesus completes the circle. He takes into his hands first the Sixth Commandment, "You shall not murder," which is stated in the Ten Commandments as a *boundary* we are warned not to cross. Jesus completes the arc to its whole intention, and in so doing we discover the Commandment's positive and greater purpose. Jesus enables us to see that the true goal of this holy commandment is that we are to honor the neighbor as a person who deserves more than mere protection against possible violence.

Beyond Murder

Jesus teaches us that we are to be reconciled to the neighbor with whom we have a grievance. We are not to take any person's dignity lightly; in fact, our very relationship with God is affected by our relationship with our neighbor. "Leave your gift . . . first go and be reconciled. . . ." Jesus has drawn the full circle, and what was previously thought of as the transgression of a boundary is now seen in positive relational terms.

I believe Jesus has a subtle purpose in his choice of such a "small" offense ("Anyone who says, 'You fool!' ") to illustrate the violation of the Sixth Commandment. By the apparent smallness of this example, Jesus has shattered the technical legalism we so often employ to excuse ourselves and to find loopholes. When the Law is seen primarily in a boundary sense, then the many technical questions as to what constitutes murder are very important. But Jesus here describes the profound purpose that stands behind the Sixth Commandment. We are not to murder because of the deep, inner worthiness God has willed for every human life. But more than that, it is God's intention and design that we are to be reconciled with our enemy.

Jesus is not therefore so interested ethically in the technical determination of the violence boundary as he is in the positive strategy we, as his disciples, should employ to break through the destructive barriers of hatred. He does much more than warn us not to murder; he challenges us to introduce a new ingredient into the old patterns of human fears, hatred, and violence. We are to be peacemakers with those whom we thought were our deadly foes.

Beyond Adultery

The Seventh Commandment, "You shall not commit adultery," is handled by Jesus in a similar way. He makes it impossible to hold to a minimal, boundary approach to marriage privileges and obligations. This is the result of his overwhelming statement, "If your right eye causes you to sin. . . ."

Many people are genuinely confused and troubled by such strong language from Jesus. We ask the question: Is in fact our Lord advocating that his disciples should literally maim their bodies in order to preserve fidelity in relationships? If he doesn't intend that we should follow such severe advice literally, then what does he intend?

This form of strong-statement teaching was not unfamiliar to Jesus' listeners. The Old Testament prophets often made use of just this kind of overwhelming language, and it is also common throughout the Psalms. For example, in Isaiah 1 the Lord tells his people through the prophet that because of their sinfulness, he will not hear them. " 'When you spread forth your hands, I will hide my eyes from you; even though you make many prayers, I will not listen. . . .' " But two verses later the Lord says, " 'Come now, let us reason together . . .' " (Isa. 1:15, 18).

Jeremiah speaks the same overwhelming language in the name of the Lord. " 'Your hurt is incurable, and your wound is grievous.' " However, within that very passage comes this sentence: " 'For I will restore health to you, and your wounds I will heal, says the Lord . . .' " (Jer. 30:12, 17). In both cases it is not correct to say that the Lord did not mean the first words. Rather, what we see in these passages is, to use Karl Barth's phrase, the "total help over against total need" of the gospel. Because of sin, our hurt is indeed incurable—apart from the total help of God's grace.

The same overwhelming language appears in the New Testament, too. Consider the language of rebuke in Revelation 3: "I will spew you out . . ." and over against these words of apparent total rejection just four verses later come the words "I stand at the door and knock; if any one hears my voice and opens the door, I will come in to him and eat with him . . .' " (Rev. 3:16, 20). Jesus on one occasion challenges his beloved friend Peter with the words, " 'Get behind me, Satan! You are a hindrance to me; for you are not on the side of God, but of men' " (Matt. 16:23). Here is another example of the hyperbole of strong language, which, by its overpowering nature, shocks Peter into facing up squarely to the real mission of Jesus Christ.

In the Sermon on the Mount Jesus has preserved the worth and meaning of human personality and human relationships. The language about the eye and hand now shocks the listener so that we might recognize how very high are the stakes in our human relationships. Our whole selfhood is involved in the sins of adultery. Unfaithfulness toward the commitment made in marriage has profound and far-reaching implications. The harm of unfaithfulness damages every relationship and every part of the whole. Jesus has startled us into really thinking through these implications by raising the possibility that it would be better to lose a hand than to lose your whole self. The net result of this teaching is not the devaluation of the hand or eye, or any part of the body, but just the opposite. We now see how very important each part of our life is. Theft in a grocery store by the highly trained stealing hand has far-reaching implications for the whole person. We are a complex whole, and each part affects every other part. That is the central teaching of this passage.

Jesus' intention for the privilege of marriage does not include divorce. Divorce cuts across the will of God for marriage. We will not learn from Jesus the technical boundary cracks or loopholes by which to justify divorce, except for the sin of unfaithfulness. In this instance, as we have noted before, our Lord has completed the arc and has shown us the circle as he intends it to be. We now have the holy will of God before us for this very intimate relationship of our lives.

This means that those of us in the human family who experience the tragedy of divorce do not hear from Jesus a legalistic measuring scale for evaluation. Rather, Jesus has taken a total approach so that as with any other crisis experience in our encounter with God's will for human life— whether the Sixth Commandment forbidding murder or in that commanding truthfulness, or some other—we who are in crisis have experienced from Jesus an intensifying of our crisis. We must not seek for help in technicalities of the observance of Law, but in the Lord who is able to heal the whole as he fulfills the whole. It is his healing and forgiveness that we need to open new possibilities of relationship for us, not the provision of legal exception or excuse. Jesus has closed off the one pathway and opened the one that leads to himself.

Beyond Oaths

The third example that Jesus notes is not a commandment from the Law of Mount Sinai; instead, it comes from the expansion of the Law found in Leviticus and Numbers: " 'You shall not swear by my name falsely . . .' " (Lev. 19:12) and " 'When a man vows a vow . . .' " (Num. 30:2). In this case, as in the others, Jesus continues to radically simplify the circle. Yet in that simplification, the arc has still been brought around to its fulfillment. The ancient purpose of vows was to insure the telling of the truth. So Jesus states it simply and plainly, "Let your 'Yes' be 'Yes,' and your 'No,' 'No.' "

How are we affected by what our Lord has said in these instances? First, we are encouraged and impressed by the high view of our own worth and the worth of others. Jesus has put into focus the meaning of life from the standpoint of his teaching and how it is meant to be lived: the neighbor we meet is to be honored by our concern to live in harmony; marriage is at last not simply in name or in a technical sense, but in the wholeness of fidelity, loyalty, and love of body, of act, and of eye—inner feeling as well as outer fact. Integrity is God's will for our speech, and therefore the ritual of oaths is not necessary to prove it.

Jesus Christ has shown to us the true sense of the vertical, and as we read these words we are profoundly impressed by that grand vertical of God's will for human life and style of life. Down deep in our consciences we know that what Jesus says is true, and that inner awareness makes his words both better than other words and harder to follow because of our own human weakness. What he has shown in even these three commandments is the way of happiness, and we know it is true even if we cannot find the way ourselves.

What has happened to us is that we have a double experience; if we are encouraged, we are also dismayed by how very hard his words are to follow. His words, like his sinless life, now stand against us. They destroy any illusions we have tried to maintain concerning our own success with the holy commandments of God. The Sermon on the Mount is therefore as discouraging as it is heartening.

The most important question is this: Is Jesus aware of the crisis he has caused for those who are really listening to his words? I believe Jesus is fully aware of this crisis. In fact, now we are able to really understand the pastoral intent of the opening promises of the sermon. Blessed are the *poor* in spirit; blessed are the *meek;* blessed are the *hungry.* If ever we were aware of the meaning of poorness, grief, meekness, and hunger for the character and the encouraging love of God, it is now, after just three of our Lord's commands. We can be thankful that it is Jesus who is speaking. The good news in the profoundest sense in the Sermon on the Mount is to be found in the one who is preaching the sermon.

5
A NEW WAY

You have heard that it was said, "An eye for an eye and a tooth for a tooth." But I say to you, Do not resist one who is evil. But if any one strikes you on the right cheek, turn to him the other also; and if any one would sue you and take your coat, let him have your cloak as well; and if any one forces you to go one mile, go with him two miles. Give to him who begs from you, and do not refuse him who would borrow from you.

You have heard that it was said, "You shall love your neighbor and hate your enemy." But I say to you, Love your enemies and pray for those who persecute you, so that you may be sons of your Father who is in heaven; for he makes his sun rise on the evil and on the good, and sends rain on the just and on the unjust. For if you love those who love you, what reward have you? Do not even the tax collectors do the same? And if you salute only your brethren, what more are you doing than others? Do not even the Gentiles do the same? You, therefore, must be perfect, as your heavenly Father is perfect.

(Matt. 5:38–48)

Jesus quotes now another text from the expansion of the
Law found in Leviticus. It was meant to limit runaway retribution and community punishment of offenders. It was also
a law for Israel that insured that only the community may
punish a wrongdoer. Personal retribution was disallowed.
"If anyone injures his neighbor, whatever he has done must
be done to him: fracture for fracture, eye for eye, tooth
for tooth" (Lev. 24:19, 20)—but no more than that.

Jesus now proposes a creative new way that dares to
break with the ancient rule of reciprocity which is a fundamental juridical principle. "Hold still," Jesus tells his disciples. "Stay in close; put a new ingredient alongside the
old, vicious cycle of retribution; go with him two miles."
This new way fulfills God's intention for life, introducing
a new power into the helplessness of an ancient crisis. It
preserves God's own right to be the judge and makes the
disciple a reconciler instead of a prosecutor or executioner.

Jesus makes it clear that the way of the reconciler is difficult and will involve unusual skill and balance. Jesus' words
do not describe the strategy of weakness but the restrained
wisdom of a person who is fully aware of what is happening
and of how potentially dangerous are the results when un-
thinking anger responds to anger in a crisis. The strategy
Jesus advocates will require tremendous skill and inner resources. It is something like the threat facing a person who
has achieved a black belt in karate when confronted by a
foe. The fact is that the better trained you are the longer
you are able to restrain yourself from an action or reaction.
In the same way it is the highly trained soldier or policeman
who is less likely than the more poorly trained officer to
blunder into physical attack. Our Lord is teaching about
a level of training and inner authority that exceeds anything
we know of in human relationship analogies—whether of
karate or peacemaking. These peacemakers are to creatively
hold their ground, to turn the cheek.

Jesus now surprises his disciples with a totally new command. They are to love the enemy and even to pray for

him. Notice that in both examples of this section of the Sermon on the Mount, Jesus is aware of the less-than-ideal setting in which his disciples must live their lives; Jesus recognizes the reality of violence, hostility, and the existence of enemies. Nevertheless the Lord shows the true shape and demand of God's holy design. The profound rightness of what Jesus is teaching becomes more compelling precisely because of the crisis he has created for all who read this sermon.

The Immense Force of God's Love

The Apostle Paul gives us a fascinating commentary on the peacemaking strategy that Jesus is teaching here. "Bless those who persecute you; bless and do not curse. . . . 'If your enemy is hungry, feed him; if he is thirsty, give him drink; for by so doing you will heap burning coals upon his head.' Do not be overcome by evil, but overcome evil with good" (Rom. 12:14, 20, 21). Paul makes two major points in his commentary on Christ's command:

1. When we dare to break the old expectations of terror for terror and rather introduce the new ingredient of meaningful love ("bless"), the result is powerfully effective because we have invoked the immense force of God's love. In fact, Paul quotes Proverbs 25 to prove his point. Love actually has the power to create a new reality, whereas punishment, at best, only fences in by force the offender and keeps him or her away from the community. Societies must make use of such threats because of human sinfulness, but Jesus gives a creative alternative for the one who has the goal of reconciliation and healing.

2. Paul's use of the word *bless* points to a thoughtful, clearheaded, and tough love that is as wise as it is well intentioned. He wants a love that knows its way, is streetwise, and helps a chaotic person find the right path. It is a love that gives drink to the thirsty enemy. How very subtle this all is! Most human sinfulness involves deep hungers and thirsts that are not being met, emptiness that is

being stuffed with false foods. Jesus challenges us to stand
our ground in the face of chaos with skill and resources
that come from our relationship with the Lord of the sermon, and then to offer those healing resources.

Even the mention of "burning coals" by Paul in his commentary on the Lord's command reinforces this. Barbara
Bowen explains in her book, *Strange Scriptures that Perplex
the Western Mind,* that people in the Middle East carried
almost everything on their heads—water jars, baskets of
fruit, vegetables, fish, and even the little braziers which
heated most homes. If your fire went out, you'd pick up
your brazier and go to your neighbor for some hot coals
to get started again. Anyone kind enough to heap coals
into your container was generous indeed. In the same way
we are to extend warmth and life to others, even our
enemies.

At the timberline of Mount Shasta, California, lives a
remarkable tree called the Shasta Fir (*Abbies magnifica, sha-
stinis*). In its early life it is twisted and almost brushlike.
The heavy snowpack, which often amounts at timberline
to more than twenty feet during the winter months, batters
and presses the young plants so that they twist and turn
and struggle to survive. There comes a winter, however,
when this tree is able to establish itself through the snowpack—and begins to point skyward like an arrow. Once
this victory is won against and through the snow, its vertical
straightness is then unmatched by any other alpine tree.
The tree is all the more impressive in the summer when
you see the twisted and oddly shaped parts of the lower
trunk. The snowpack has done its best to distort and crowd
and harass, but when the time is right, the Shasta Fir wins
out over the crushing weight of the snow and gale force
winds. The vertical is all the more impressive in the face
of the odds against it.

The way of costly love is no less impressive. We wonder
how it possibly could work in our own particular stormy
and windy situations. On the other hand, we know from

our journey through life and the history of civilizations that the ways of retaliation and hatred for enemies have inevitably led to the widening of hatreds and finally to war. That track record is obvious. The way of Christ's love has a track record too.

The Creative Way of Self-Limitation

Jesus has advocated the creative way of self-limitation. This depends upon God's healing and redeeming power to make it work. It is a way that counts upon the completion of the Torah's grand intentions by God, so that the great power of love overrides the power of retribution and animosity.

Aleksandr Solzhenitsyn puts these principles into contemporary focus in the following way:

> We are always very ready to limit others—that is what all politicians are engaged in . . . We are always anxiously on the lookout for ways of curbing the inordinate greed of the *other man,* but no one is heard renouncing his *own* inordinate greed. . . . The idea of self-limitation in society is not a new one. We find it a century ago in such thoroughgoing Christians as the Russian old believers.[1]

Solzhenitsyn goes on to argue that it is this very self-limitation practiced by the "thoroughgoing Christians" that our twentieth century needs more than any other social virtue. It should not only be practiced by individuals but also by nations! It is the only way that nuclear deescalation of weapons will happen.

Jesus challenges his disciples to dare such a good strategy of hope. Self-limitation should never be seen as passive or the strategy of inactivity. Jesus is describing a strategy of dynamic *action* aimed at breaking through the old patterns of fear. It involves finding the real person who hides behind old patterns. The new strategy of Jesus has the immense power of his authority to back it up, and it is this holy power Paul refers to in Romans 12:21, "Do not be overcome by evil, but overcome evil with good." It requires skill and wisdom to carry out this new strategy; most of all, it requires confidence that over the long run the power of good outlasts the power of fear.

We must also note one more very important fact. When Jesus tells his disciples to "love your enemies and pray for those who persecute you," he is stating a theological reality even deeper than the outward advice about strategy toward the world. Jesus' advice will really work only because Jesus is able to forgive and make whole the man or woman who is the persecutor. This means that we, as his disciples, ought not to view any person as a lost cause or as someone beyond the reach of Christ's love. This confidence on our part as twentieth-century peacemakers makes it all work.

Additional Notes

The Levitical setting for Retribution Law, "Eye for eye . . .", is so designed to eliminate the possibility of personal vengeance. Only the community has the privilege of punishment of wrongdoers and that only after hearings with witnesses.

It is also the intention of the Levitical code to ensure the principle of equal justice under law—"You shall do no injustice in judgment; you shall not be partial to the poor or defer to the great, but in righteousness shall you judge your neighbor" (Lev. 19:15). Jesus does not repudiate these principles of community justice as he calls his disciples to move beyond them toward a richer possibility.

6
SECRETS

Beware of practicing your piety before men in order to be seen by them; for then you will have no reward from your Father who is in heaven.

Thus, when you give alms, sound no trumpet before you, as the hypocrites do in the synagogues and in the streets, that they may be praised by men. Truly, I say to you, they have their reward. But when you give alms, do not let your left hand know what your right hand is doing, so that your alms may be in secret; and your Father who sees in secret will reward you.

And when you pray, you must not be like the hypocrites; for they love to stand and pray in the synagogues and at the street corners, that they may be seen by men. Truly, I say to you, they have their reward. But when you pray, go into your room and shut the door and pray to your Father who is in secret; and your Father who sees in secret will reward you.

And when you fast, do not look dismal, like the hypocrites, for they disfigure their faces that their fasting may be seen by men. Truly, I say to you, they have their reward. But when you fast, anoint your head and wash your face, that your fasting may not be seen by men but by your Father who is in secret; and your Father who sees in secret will reward you.

(Matt. 6:1–6, 16–18)

Jesus now poses several sets of apparent contradictions. At the opening of his sermon, he plainly commanded his followers, " 'Let your light so shine before men, that they may see your good works . . .' " (Matt. 5:16). In chapter 6 he says, "Beware of practicing your piety before men, in order to be seen by them. . . ." In one place he teaches, "Let your light shine," and then in these sentences of chapter 6 he says, "Keep it all a secret."

This contrast of revelation first as proclamation and then as secret was something Jesus not only taught but also demonstrated in his own ministry. On the one side, he was the Light of the world, and said so more than once (John 8:12; 9:5; 12:35, 36). Yet this same Jesus Christ baffled his disciples on countless occasions by keeping his Messianic secret. "Perceiving then that they were about to come and take him by force to make him king, Jesus withdrew again to the hills by himself" (John 6:15).

Three Reasons

Why does he talk and behave this way? Is it possible to unite the contrasting mandates of Matthew 6 and Matthew 5?

Here are three reasons, as I see it, for the command to keep secrets:

1. Jesus wants his disciples to experience the acts of righteousness for their *own* sake, free from public interference. He promises that the ultimate joy of sharing money, for example, will be granted to those who share only when uncluttered by press releases.

Prayer is the act of relationship. To enter into what prayer is all about, *keep it personal.* Prayer as a sincere interchange with the Lord who knows you and loves you will then become your discovery and your experience of relationship.

On the subject of acts of discipline, such as fasting, his counsel again results in a sharpening of the focus and basic purpose of the particular act of discipline. Fasting is to aid in our spiritual growth; it may help to clarify our priorities and enable us to use the money thereby saved to aid the poor. Jesus' command is this: your acts of discipline are between you and your Lord. Let the neighbor benefit from the healthy result of spiritual formation and growth within your life, but as for the rigors of your journey toward that growth, don't mention it. "Wash your face," Jesus tells his disciples, so the people around you will not know of your hard work in their behalf. It is clear from this teaching that Jesus has in mind a direct connection between discipline and health. Privation and self-denial that result in a sickly and weakened disciple has very little positive result for a world that needs healthy priorities and healthy people to make these servant priorities happen.

2. There is another reason for Jesus' command to refrain from any public display of acts of piety. Jesus enables us by this counsel to understand who we are as individuals in relationship with God. For a human being to be truly human, it is very important that he or she have a sense of the secret of the self. Jesus honors this inner mystery about what it means to be fully human. In the light of this perspective, we are able to appreciate the interior, very private, personal nature of the Beatitudes. "Poor in spirit . . . mourn . . . meek . . . hunger and thirst for righteousness"—each of these is set within the most intimate inner part of our self understanding. They are not words that express the rush of sensory stimulation.

Throughout his ministry our Lord was a revealer of what was hidden within selfhood, as in the interview with the Samaritan woman (John 4 "Where is your husband?"). At the same time, however, Jesus was the great preserver of the mystery of each man or woman. He was unwilling to compel the rich young ruler to believe either by argument or proof (Mark 10). Jesus Christ does not take away our freedom to decide the most important decisions by the sweep of his awesome authority which could and would overwhelm our decision-making processes. In fact, his authority is demonstrated precisely in the way he sets free those who accept his lordship, and even in the way he preserves the freedom of those who refuse his reign.

C. S. Lewis's Screwtape, the senior devil in *The Screwtape Letters,* cannot understand why this should be so. The senior devil writes about this mystery to Wormwood: "You must have often wondered why the Enemy does not make more use of His power. . . . But you see now that the Irresistible and the Indisputable are the two weapons which the very nature of His Scheme forbids Him to use. Merely to override a human will . . . would be for Him useless . . . merely to cancel them, or assimilate them, will not serve. . . ." [1] Screwtape cannot understand why God preserves our human secrets and our right to the freedom of secrets.

3. In my view the third reason for the secrecy mandate is that it prepares us for truly meaningful relationships with our neighbor. Notice that the Beatitudes proceeded from the interior self-perception of mourning and meekness to the interpersonal and social result of mercy and peacemaking. In the same way the ethical challenge of the gospel always moves from the prior fact of our own personal sense of "belovedness" toward the dynamic implication of "let us love one another."

Need for Secrecy

Paul Tournier has brought into focus some of the psychological aspects of this theological point. He writes, "Every human being needs secrecy in order to become himself and no longer a member of his tribe . . . in order to collect his thoughts. . . . To respect the secrecy of whoever it may be, even your own child, is to respect his individuality. To intrude upon his private life, to violate his secrecy, is to violate his individuality." [2]

Later in the same book Tournier also writes: "So, therefore, if keeping a secret was the first step in the formation of the individual, telling it to a freely chosen confidant is going to constitute then the second step in this formation of the individual. . . . He who cannot keep a secret is not free. But he who can never reveal it is not free either." [3]

Jesus has drawn together both the need for the secret and the need for the open sharing of righteousness. Both mandates are marks of a Christian style of life. The disciple-ship challenge that now faces us as we want to live by the Sermon on the Mount is to do both at the same time. We are to give, pray, and fast without regard for the appreci-ation of others. At the same moment we are to act as lamp-stands, or citadel cities, with all the lights turned on, so that our generation of wanderers, lost and confused in the heavy fog, may find the way to the source of love. What Jesus has done by this double mandate in the Sermon on the Mount is to clarify the motivations of his disciples. The mandates, though they appear contradictory, are really profoundly dependent upon each other. They go together. We should not act or speak too quickly; we should be first still in our journey of prayer, and we should practice quietly the spiritual lessons we are learning. But we must not always sit quietly, restrained by contemplation and secret prayer. There is a time to speak and there is a time to act. The point is that if we have had the quiet time alone with God we will be better enabled to keep our decisive appointment with action and proclamation.

Additional Notes

Note that Jesus says, "*When* you give alms . . . *when* you fast . . ." not *if.* Jesus sharply criticizes hypocrisy but not the acts of *fasting* or *almsgiving* or *prayer.* Martin Luther puts Jesus' perspective into theological focus for us concern-ing these religious acts: "But by all means not for the pur-pose of making an act of worship out of it, to merit something by it, or to propitiate God . . ." (*Lectures on the Sermon on the Mount,* Martin Luther, p. 276). Luther goes on to say of prayer, "The Christian prays, and because he knows that God hears him, he does not need to prate everlastingly. Thus the saints in the Scripture prayed with short, but strong and powerful words" (p. 249). "The error of the hypocrite is selfishness . . . the error of the heathen is meaninglessness," says John R. W. Stott.

7

A PRAYER FOR
ALL SEASONS

And in praying do not heap up empty phrases as the Gentiles do; for they think that they will be heard for their many words. Do not be like them, for your Father knows what you need before you ask him. Pray then like this:

Our Father who art in heaven,
Hallowed be thy name.
Thy kingdom come,
Thy will be done,
On earth as it is in heaven.
Give us this day our daily bread. . . .

(Matt. 6:7–11)

Right at the heart of Jesus' teaching on the secret way of personal righteousness, he shares a simple prayer that we now want to consider. It is a brief prayer, with only four sentences. It is personal, yet it is plural; it has a universal ring to it, and yet it honors human uniqueness and individuality. But first, before Jesus teaches a prayer for us to repeat, he speaks a warning as the preface to the prayer, a warning against empty phrases with many words. Scholars of the first century have been able to help us understand this reference of Jesus to pagan prayers. The Greco-Roman mystery cult religions that dominated the first-century Mediterranean world had a chaotic excess of words and ritual. In the city of Pergamum alone there were several temples built for emperor worship, as well as temples to Zeus, Asclepius, Athena, and Dionysus. Citizens were expected to worship at all of these temples. Tacitus, the Roman historian, admits that many Romans and Greeks in the first century turned toward Jewish religion precisely because they were attracted by its absence of excessive words, statues, and rituals. The Law, Psalms, and prophetic writings of the Old Testament stand in sharp contrast to the prayers and poems of the pagan religions at this point. Prayers in the Old Testament are uncomplicated, nonrepetitious, and nonmagical.

We have a fascinating clue in the New Testament to this contrast. During the riot of the silversmiths in Ephesus, the angry crowd chanted nonstop for two hours, " 'Great is Artemis of the Ephesians!' " (Acts 19:34). They couldn't think of anything else to say! But what they could think of they repeated endlessly.

Jesus makes it clear that God is not honored by such repetition. We do not need to remind God continuously of his existence and his greatness, nor do we need to repeat our requests obsessively. God is our Father, and he knows us well. The theological and psychological implications of Jesus' statements about prayer are very important. He has shown us that neither emotional nor intellectual intensity is a guarantee of truth; the amount a person speaks or feels is not the test of reality, but rather the trustworthiness of the one to whom our devotion is directed. Luther would like this prayer Jesus now teaches to his disciples because it is "short, strong, and with powerful words."

The preface to the prayer concludes with the deeply encouraging reminder that the one to whom we pray cares so deeply about us that we may call him Father. Can we appreciate the surprise Jesus' listeners must have felt at the use of the word *Father?* The Pharisee movement in first-century Judaism had taken a very narrow interpretation of the Third Commandment, " 'You shall not take the name of the Lord your God in vain' " (Ex. 20:7). Their practice was to avoid all direct reference to God and especially any use of the holy name *Yahweh.* Indirect forms of expression were preferred as signs of reverence. In view of this hesitancy, we are all the more struck by our Lord's informality and even intimacy, which he endorses to his followers as the proper and worshipful way to pray.

Though first-century Jews were not accustomed to the intimate term *Father* the fact is that Jesus by this warm and personal term returned his listeners to an older tradition behind the highly artificial reticence of the Pharisee movement toward the holy name of God. Just as the name *Yahweh* is used frequently in the Old Testament (5,500 times) so *Father* is also common in Old Testament usage. The intensely personal word *Father* is used in the Old Testament to describe God's relationship to his people. Israel is reminded in Deuteronomy 32:6 " 'Is not he your father, who created you. . . .' " The prophet Isaiah cries out in prayer to God, ". . . thou art our Father . . ." (Isa. 63:16). Jeremiah knew God in the same way: " 'And I thought you would call me, My Father . . .' " (Jer. 3:19). Malachi 1:6 has a haunting question that comes from God toward his people: " 'If then I am a father, where is my honor. . . .' " In the intertestamental Book of Wisdom there is a very important Messianic prophecy: "He calls the last end of the righteous happy, and boasts that God is his father" (Wisdom 2:16).

Jesus fulfilled the expectation of the writer of the Book of Wisdom and according to John's account Jesus claimed this intimate term *Father* in the most complete sense. In an argument with the Pharisees recorded in John 8 Jesus tells them " 'You know neither me nor my Father; if you knew me, you would honor my Father also' " (John 8:19). But Jesus did not only claim this word for himself; he also invited those who would hear the Sermon on the Mount to approach God with the same word. In Gethsemane, according to Mark's account, our Lord made use of the even more personal and affectionate Aramaic expression "Abba." Jesus said, " 'Abba, Father, all things are possible to thee; remove this cup from me; yet not what I will, but what thou wilt' " (Mark 14:36). Paul tells us that this very affectionate and intimate term is given to each one of us as well if we reach out toward God: ". . . you have received the spirit of sonship. When we cry, 'Abba! Father!' " (Rom. 8:15).

What is important for us to see in these opening two words of this prayer is that Jesus reestablishes the felt sense of closeness to God which was the mark of the prophets and the psalmists, but which had been suppressed in the life of Israel from the time of the Maccabean revolt onward, especially by the Pharisee movement. This means that from about 156 B.C. to the time of our Lord's ministry the prayers of Israel had become more specialized, formal, and kingdom-oriented and less personal, less intimate.

Let me explore now the first two of the prayer's four main parts.

A Prayer for the Kingdom of God

Before anything else, Jesus teaches us to address God as Father, and then to acknowledge God's holiness—to ask for his reign upon the earth. The Kingdom of God is seen in the New Testament in relationship terms, not territorial terms. The Kingdom is where the King and his subjects are. By his own sovereign decision the King of all creation has created the very earth itself, and has sustained the earth; he redeems the earth and fulfills its destiny. So before all other requests, Jesus invites us to pray, "O God, we seek first of all your presence as Lord." Or to put it another way: "O God, grant your reign as the solid ground beneath everything else." It is a prayer for the eternal Alpha and Omega as the one place or ground where we may stand and build our lives. Jesus is right in making this the very first request because apart from this rock there is no hope nor any reason for the making of prayers.

Unlike the Jewish rabbinical document, the Kaddish, there is no mention of Israel in connection with this Kingdom prayer. It is rather the more generic sense of kingdom that is signaled by the way the words unfold. Kingdom is where the King is and this prayer asks for the reign of the King.

At the beginning of my own study of the Lord's Prayer this opening request was difficult for me to really understand at a personal level. It seemed to me at the early stages of my own reflection that it would make better sense to place these words at the close of the prayer. There is an eschatological feeling about them that would have been, I thought, more psychologically appropriate at the conclusion of a series of practical requests. This would then surround the earthy and urgent requests for survival, forgiveness, and protection from evil with the yearning for the coming of the King.

But in fact, and contrary to my own preferences, our Lord instructed his disciples as follows: *Before you pray for anything else pray this:* "Thy kingdom come, thy will be done, on earth as it is in heaven." *Pray for the presence of God* before you pray for anything else. The question is, what does this really mean in terms of our lives both practically and theologically? Is Jesus accurate in his understanding of human beings to conclude that this prayer would be, in the real world where people live, the first earnest petition on our minds and hearts? Is Jesus realistic about the concerns of the disciples and their priorities of concern, or is he teaching his disciples that this is what they *ought* to pray regardless of the urgency scale they know in their own human experience? In my own journey with this text I asked these puzzling questions and when the pieces of the puzzle came together I realized that Jesus was as wonderfully accurate in the *order* of his prayer as he is in the final *content* of the prayer. I am convinced that our Lord is faithful to the human urgency scale and therefore these words are not simply liturgically placed where they are. They are also realistically placed right here.

Let me offer an illustration to show what I mean in psychological terms.

Imagine that you are a British officer present at the annual Hong Kong Crown Colony Military Garrison Christmas Ball; it is December 1941 and the ball is held, as it has been traditionally, in the beautiful lobby of the Peninsula Hotel. Let us suppose that you are one of the young British officers at that party; all of the separate parts of your life are successful and positive. You have a happy family, a loving wife, a recent grade promotion in the Royal Navy, a sound income and retirement plan. The occasion is luxurious and cheerful with friends, and the atmosphere is that of a festive party. But you feel sick inside. It is not caused by any failure or wrongness with the parts of your life, nevertheless the sick feeling of ennui is there. You have that feeling of ennui because you know that the ground beneath everything is deteriorating and beginning to break apart. You are aware that the earthquake of a world war is about to begin. It is the shaking of the foundations that now causes your fears. Such a Christmas grand ball did in fact entertain British society in Hong Kong on the eve of the conflict of World War II that was to overrun East Asia, and perhaps not a few officers and wives felt this strange uneasiness of the failure of foundations.

This profound worry about the ground beneath everything is the profoundest anxiety known to humankind. It is the fear of a small child lost in a park who though now safe at the park police station still sobs from the intensely existential fear that the earth beneath his or her very existence which the mother and father represent has been lost. The parts are all in good condition—ice cream cone, TV set is on, the police officers, though strangers, are friendly—but the shudder of fear has to do with a primeval anxiety about the ground beneath everything. This ache is as real today in our twentieth century as it was in the century of the Roman Empire. The ache persists even though the separate parts are impressive. The ache persists in spite of all human schemes to divert our attention away from the awareness or to repress the anxiety. Materialism and spiritualism are both in their own ways desperate forms of denial of the real fear. "We cling . . . but nothing stays for us" (Pascal).

Jesus Christ taught his hearers to pray a very basic prayer—the most basic prayer—at the heart of the Sermon on the Mount: "Before you pray for anything else, pray this—'Oh God, grant first of all a solid ground beneath everything.' "

I believe this is the first request of the Lord's Prayer, "Thy kingdom come. . . ." This is the prayer for the foundation that is strong enough to bear the weight of everything—even wars that tear apart families and nations and also children lost in the park.

Before we pray for bread or for forgiveness we pray for the ground of God's character and reign to stand beneath the separate parts. Jesus Christ is not only the earth's Redeemer; he is the earth's Sustainer. This is therefore the most urgent prayer because it is the prayer that faces up to the shaking of the foundations. "One may face many things cynically . . . but there is one thing we cannot be cynical about and that is the shaking of the foundations of everything" (Paul Tillich).

This means, theologically, that the Christian is being taught by Jesus to live now in the present by the fact that

Jesus Christ himself boundaries history at its origin, at its center, and at its end. This prayer is eschatological and at the same time profoundly present tense and existential. It is most of all a *prayer* and since our Lord teaches us to pray such a prayer we have confidence that what he has invited us to pray he will grant. Therefore the practical implication of this first petition is that we are given a basis for genuine optimism, for hope concerning the separate parts of our lives as well as the ground that stands beneath the parts.

A Prayer for Human Survival

The second part of the prayer is contained in one sentence; it is the essence of directness and practical immediacy. "Give us this day our daily bread." Jesus invites us to share with God our concerns for the very earthy, basic parts of human existence, the physical ingredients we need for survival. Notice that in these six simple words Jesus runs cross-grain to the premises of *two* world views: the materialistic and the spiritualistic.

1. Materialism is the iron embrace of the world. It believes that a person gains meaning for his or her life from the material items of the world and the experiences that go with those concrete items. In some instances and in certain forms of materialism as a philosophy of life and world view this includes the person among those material ingredients of the whole. Materialism leads inevitably to the conclusion that ownership grants meaning. The parts of existence—houses, land, persons, even the relationships that involve these parts—are then treated as objects to be owned and possessed. The criterion for the good life is simple enough: What are you able to buy and own?

Jesus Christ challenges that premise by putting the physical parts of life into a larger whole. These concrete parts of life are gifts from the God who cares about our real existence. Jesus also places these parts into a daily context. Each day we need bread. Like every part of the creation, bread is limited. Therefore, the theological implication of this prayer is that when the meaning of our life becomes founded upon any part or collection of parts of the created order, it is then rooted in too small a place. The parts themselves belong to a larger whole. In this way Jesus grants meaning to the logical and real need of human beings to physically survive. These actual parts are not discounted by Jesus or treated with contempt, but they are treated as ingredients of the whole and not the end of the whole. They are gifts from God and therefore their intrinsic meaning, their specific gravity, does not come from themselves but from their original and greater source. We cannot know their true weight when we treat them otherwise. The fatal flaw of both capitalism as an end in itself or communism as an end in itself is the resulting materialistic devotion to the physical parts of the whole.

Secondly, Jesus puts the physical ingredients of life into a daily context. We need them each day, which is the true nature of their urgency; yet by that very descriptive limitation each of the parts of the created order is itself limited and not final in itself, because only God himself stands beyond the boundary of "our daily bread." When we mean what we say in this second petition of the Our Father Prayer, then we are set free from the tyranny of the parts to become stewards of the parts. When this prayer becomes the actual conviction of our lives then we are not as possessive as before, not as edgy, not as desperate, and that is what I mean by the expression "set free."

The prayer is not an argument against hard work for bread nor is it an argument against responsibility toward the earth. The awareness of stewardship this petition implies always has the effect of increasing our sense of respect for the parts because we know of their good origin as a meaningful part of God's design and intention for the earth.

The materialist is tempted toward the direction of a careless and headlong ownership-worship of the earth, but the earth cannot endure our worship. Whether it is the worship of the crocodile or the worship of technology, in each case the worship is misplaced and those who worship any of the parts of creation are not able to make sense of the whole of creation. The earth is to be honored and preserved because of its good origin and its goal; it must not be worshiped as if it were the origin and the goal. This earth of ours is to be fulfilled (Rom. 8:21), "Because the creation itself will be set free from its bondage to decay and obtain the glorious liberty of the children of God." This prayer is a frontal challenge to materialism because it points our eyes toward the spiritual source of all things, great and small.

2. At the same time this brief sentence in the Lord's Prayer is a surprise to the spiritualistic world view. Spiritualism would have written a different prayer than the one Jesus has taught, perhaps: "O God, help us to have supremacy of spirit over the body, so that we will no longer need the daily bread of physical and emotional support from the material world of things and people—to the end that our spirits may soar."

"Give Us Our Daily *Cake*"

During the first century, as in our own time, many people, both Jews and Greeks, would have preferred just this sort of more "spiritual" prayer. Their argument would have run as follows: First, should not our prayers lift our sights far above earth and its petty concerns? Secondly, is not the word *daily* an affront to the spiritual quest of the human spirit? Does not the spiritual goal seek to avoid if at all possible every tie to daily, ordinary, and limited life? Even "Give us our daily cake" would have been better; but bread, mere bread, as all people of every lowly station need—how commonplace and humiliating!

It is interesting to note that certain early interpreters of the Our Father Prayer thought the request was too worldly. Tertullian, Cyprian, and even Augustine were of the opinion therefore that Jesus must have been inviting his disciples to pray for more than ordinary bread. Augustine interpreted this sentence as the prayer for "the invisible bread of the word of God" (see J. R. W. Stott's discussion of this issue, *Christian Counter-Culture,* p. 148). But Augustine's interpretation is artificial and is textually unwarranted.

Jerome also advanced this view in his Latin translation of the word *epiousis* which he rendered "super-substantial." But there is no linguistic or textual basis for such a translation. Jerome and Augustine were swayed by an earnest desire to seek a "higher" spiritual meaning for a simple sentence and in so doing they adopted a luxurious rather than a lean interpretive stance toward the sentence. In questions of interpretation the wiser rule is that "lean is better than luxurious." (See the author's discussion of this interpretive principle in his volume on 1, 2, 3 John and Revelation in *The Communicator's Commentary.*)

But Jesus Christ has taught a prayer that fully understands both the material and the spiritual quest of humanity. The deepest longing of each quest is fulfilled in the prayer Jesus taught. Our change of words is not necessary to help the prayer become more spiritual or more profound.

We must ask one final question of this part of Jesus' teaching on prayer. Does believing that daily life is a gift from God make us less realistic, less creative toward our responsibilities toward ourselves and the earth around us? Would we be more creative if we were more autonomous and less dependent?

I believe the biblical view which recognizes our human position as stewards and never owners of the creation is *more* creative than either the materialistic or the spiritualistic view of life. It involves just the right degree of limitation to prevent us from making ourselves gods, and it also prevents the created order from becoming an idol of our affections and/or our fears. We are thereby set free from these two bondages and we are set free to act and be and work with the created order in a healthy relationship between our human selves and the real world around us.

Additional Notes

Prayer as practiced by the Jewish people by the time of the first century had become very nationalized and kingdom oriented. "That prayer in which there is no mention of the kingdom of God is not a prayer" (the Talmud, quoted by Alfred Plummer in his *Exegetical Commentary on the Gospel According to St. Matthew*). The discovery of the Dead Sea Scrolls has recovered for us many prayers of this period in history and they are noted for their lack of personal warmth. They are directed primarily toward technical concerns of the community and the various questions of ceremonial purity; they are prayers for war, victory, national kingdom success. This does not mean that all first-century prayers are impersonal and have become totally civic. A prayer in the first-century *Kaddish* is a personal prayer very much like the Our Father Prayer.

> May His great name be magnified and sanctified in the world which He has created according to His will. May His sovereignty reign in your life and in your days, and in the life of all the house of Israel, speedily and at a near time. And say ye amen.

Let us make some reflections on the word *kingdom* in the world of Old and New Testament thought. "One thing is certain: the word kingdom did not have for the oriental the significance that the word kingdom does for the westerner. Only in quite isolated instances in the Old Testament does *Malkut* denote a realm in the spatial sense, a territory; almost always it stands for the government, the authority, the power of a King . . . thus the reign of God is neither spatial nor a static concept; it is a *dynamic concept*. It denotes the reign of God in action. . . ." [1]

The word translated "daily" is the Greek word *epiousis* which is not only rare in its New Testament usage (it appears in the New Testament only here and in Luke's account of the Lord's Prayer). It has also only been found in one other first-century citation, and that is in a list of business expenses. Moulton and Milligan make the following observation. "The papyri have yet shed no clear light upon this difficult word which was in all probability a new coinage by the author of the Greek to render his Aramaic original." [2] Our very best clue to the sense of the word comes from a sentence in the Proverbs that appears to be a model for this part of Our Lord's Prayer: "Give me neither poverty nor riches; feed me with the food that is needful for me. . . ." This common and earthly request for today's food or for needful food is the sense of the word *epiousis* in its other ancient example of use in classical Greek, the expense list.

Therefore the view of the majority of linguistic scholars has supported the translation which we have in the RSV, "give us our daily bread."

8
THE ENORMOUS EXCEPTION

And forgive us our debts,
As we also have forgiven our debtors;

For if you forgive men their trespasses, your heavenly Father also will forgive you; but if you do not forgive men their trespasses, neither will your Father forgive your trespasses.

(Matt. 6:12, 14, 15)

"Thus it is that our effort to set the Sermon on the Mount historically in its place finally sets us in our place," says W. D. Davies. "And the place in which it sets us is the last judgement, before the infinite help and the infinite demand of Christ."

We need forgiveness because we are guilty. Notice how universal the Our Father Prayer is in its scope as each petition is universally applied. Jesus does not instruct his followers to select the petitions that are applicable. The prayer does not read, "And those who have sinned should pray thus: forgive us our debts. . . ." The assumption of Jesus' prayer is that each disciple needs to make this request for forgiveness. Some may have felt sinless at the hillside prior to the Sermon on the Mount but those who have listened to Jesus' words in chapters 5 and 6 of Matthew no longer feel sinless. Therefore this permission for our request for forgiveness comes just in time.

Jesus now invites us to ask forgiveness for our debts. The word *debts* is the most accurate translation of the Greek word used in Matthew's text. We owe God a life of obedience and righteousness, and we keep defaulting. *Debts* is thus a metaphor for the common word *sins* which Luke uses in his narration of the Lord's Prayer (Luke 11:4).

A Bargain?

Verse 12, with its two parts, is a prayer and not a bargain. It is not a petition that might sound as follows: "Lord, watch how generous we have been toward those who have offended us; now please be generous to us in view of these achieved credits that have accumulated to our benefit." It is rather, "Lord, please grant us forgiveness—something we know about and appreciate from our human experiences with one another, and help us to share the forgiveness we receive with those nearby who also need forgiveness."

Notice in verses 14 and 15 that our part comes first in the ethical implications of forgiveness: if *we* forgive, then *God* will complete forgiveness and its good result. We do not set the rules; Christ does. This ought to disqualify the kind of praying we hear occasionally: "God, if you'll just get me this job (or resolve the conflict with my parents, or whatever), then I'll serve you and do all manner of wonderful things for your Kingdom." Our relationship with God is prior to the ethical implications of the prayer; therefore, we submit to the Father in prayer.

In the Greek world of thought, prayer was understood primarily as a bargain that a mortal might make with one of the gods. The Greek root word translated by the English word *pray* is *eukomai* which means to invoke, vow, or promise. When prayer is mentioned in the New Testament, the Greek word usually used is not *eukomai* but *proseukomai*. The prefix "to" or "toward" is added by New Testament writers to signal to the reader that the word means something different than what the classical Greek usage intended. *Pros* shifts the attention toward the one to whom the prayer is made. The word, therefore, carries the literal meaning of "to pray toward." The point is clear that in both the Old and New Testament, prayer is not a vow, promise, or bargain made with God. It is the bringing of my whole self into his presence.

C. S. Lewis has captured the profound implications of this in the way he portrays Aslan's relationship with the characters in the seven stories of *The Chronicles of Narnia*. Digory, for example, in *The Magician's Nephew*, discovers the immense creative power of Aslan, the great golden Lion, Son of the Emperor from beyond the sea. But a deep worry is heavy upon Digory's heart when he remembers the grave illness of his mother, who is back in England while Digory has been caught up in his wondrous adventures in Narnia. Digory's worry is heightened because he does not know the rules of Narnia, that time spent there uses up no time in the other world of England.

Just at that point, Aslan calls to Digory to send him on a long and dangerous mission. Listen to Lewis as he narrates this encounter.

" 'Son of Adam,' said Aslan. 'Are you ready . . . ?'

" 'Yes,' said Digory. He had had for a second some wild idea of saying 'I'll try to help you if you'll promise to help about my Mother,' but he realised in time that the Lion was not at all the sort of person one could try to make bargains with. But when he had said, 'Yes' . . . a lump came in his throat and tears in his eyes, and he blurted out:

" 'But please, please—won't you—can't you give me something that will cure Mother?' "

That is precisely the Bible's teaching on prayer: we are to blurt out our true feelings, our deepest needs, to the Lord, who has invited us to do that very thing. It is in no sense a bargain; it is in every sense even more daring than a bargain. It is coming into the presence of God with our real selves and with our deepest cares.

What Does Forgiveness Mean?

Not long ago, at a national youth worker's convention, I met a young man who had spent some three years of his life in my city, Berkeley, California. He had lived as a nomadic youth, adrift and alone. He told me of how toward the final months of those three years, he had met a Christian family in our church. They befriended him, and finally through their witness, he trusted Jesus Christ as Lord. His life was radically rearranged by that experience of the healing love of Jesus following his conversion experience. He returned to his home across the country, finished school, was married, and started his own family. Now some six years later here he was, a highly motivated man in his early thirties, a husband and father. But he said something that made a very deep impression upon me: "You know, a large part of the three years I spent in Berkeley are a blur in my memory. I have shadowy recollections, but it is as if three years are just missing from my life."

Here is a young man who has experienced the forgiveness Jesus is promising in this prayer. Forgiveness does not mean he has the chance to relive the three lost years, to do them over. Some of the marks of confused days and nights on Telegraph Avenue are still visible. But what has happened to him and in him is that his past, all of it, has been resolved and reconciled by the grace of the Savior. He has been granted the chance for a genuinely new beginning, on a new footing, because of the redeeming grace of Jesus Christ. He does not have the privilege of returning to the past, or returning to innocence; but what he does receive in his repentance and the forgiveness of Jesus Christ is a new beginning right in the middle of his journey already under way.

The prayer that Jesus teaches does not leave our request for our own forgiveness as a single uncomplicated petition. The prayer creates a connection between my own experience of the forgiveness of my sinfulness and my inescapable obligation toward the sinners who surround me. The second half of this petition has been very challenging not only to those who speak the prayer but also to interpreters of the prayer who want to understand its meaning. Our Lord follows the text of the prayer with an additional sentence that further strengthens the importance of this second half of the petition: "For if you forgive men their trespasses, your heavenly Father also will forgive you; but if you do not forgive men their trespasses, neither will your Father forgive your trespasses" (Matt. 6:14, 15).

This part of the Lord's Prayer makes it plain that Jesus does not expect that his disciples will live their discipleship in an ideal setting free from the threat of sin and its harm. Jesus is fully aware of his disciples' need for forgiveness, and also that they will live their lives in places where they will encounter the sins of other people toward them.

The second part of the forgiveness prayer points up the connectedness of inner forgiveness and outer ethics as a result of forgiveness. It is very significant that this highly charged ethical demand is placed upon us as disciples in the setting of our own experience of forgiveness and the caring grace that goes with forgiveness. We have in this text the classic portrayal of what theologians describe as evangelical ethics, or what Dietrich Bonhoeffer called "formation ethics." It is the ethical mandate and possibility that grows out of fulness rather than from emptiness or guilt. We are ourselves first forgiven and then we are commanded from that fulness to express toward those around us the same forgiveness that we ourselves experienced. We are not expected to invent forgiveness from within our own resources, but we are commanded to share the forgiveness we have received. It seems to me Martin Luther in his commentary on the Sermon on the Mount has wisely caught this crucial connection: "Christ meant especially to state this petition in such a way, and to link the forgiveness of sin to our forgiving, so that hereby he would obligate the Christians to love. . . ."

After Forgiveness, What Then?

Luther continues, "See, this is the twofold forgiveness; one internal in the heart, that clings alone to the word of God; and one external, that breaks forth, and assures us that we have the internal one."

Luther's final sentence is a fascinating insight. When we forgive other people then it is by that ethical act that we experience the assurance that our own forgiveness by Jesus Christ is real. In other words we have exercised grace and have found it sufficient. Therefore, even in the commands of Jesus we find the good news of Jesus. It means in practical terms that if we want to be more certain of God's love we should risk it more often and then we would see how real that love is.

"Thus the words of the Sermon on the Mount ultimately lead us back to Him who uttered them," says Davies. "Its imperatives thus become indicatives. . . . This is why nowhere in the New Testament is the Gospel set forth without moral demand, and nowhere is morality understood apart from the Gospel." When we meet that one who speaks these words and teaches this prayer we meet the one who makes forgiveness possible because Jesus Christ himself has fulfilled this prayer. Forgiveness is possible because of the identification of Christ with us; without Jesus Christ the Savior there would be no forgiveness. Each of the requests in the Lord's Prayer reach out toward the kingly reign of Christ and this is a request that reaches out for resolution, by the Lord of the Kingdom, of a complicated moral and spiritual crisis.

The crisis of human sinfulness is so tightly interconnected with who we are and what we fear, the desires that motivate life and the real harm that we have become involved in that the resolution of such a crisis takes the total help of the one who created us. The prayer for forgiveness asks for that total help and because the power of that help is so profoundly far-reaching, it is understandable how this request should break out from the forgiveness we have received and be expressed by us toward those around us. We cannot have one without the other because the power of forgiveness is so great. Karl Barth describes forgiveness as the power of powers. It is the discovery that God is for me!

This personal experience is so completely life changing that it radically alters everything—my self view, my understanding of other people, my ethics, my emotions. Because of God's forgiveness there must be a celebration, as in the story Jesus told of the return of the prodigal. The joy that is created by forgiveness is too radically and totally good to keep as a secret. Forgiveness creates the celebration because of its surprise. Just when we were convinced of our hopeless entrapment and downward slide into condemnation and despair we are confronted instead by acceptance and the love that knows how to cope with failures and how to heal the memories of failure. Because of this good surprise in the good news we are invited to the grand party of the Father. "This my son was dead but now he is alive."

General Oglethorpe said to John Wesley, "I never forgive."

Wesley replied, "Then I hope, Sir, you never sin."

The poor general is like the lonely elder brother in Jesus' story. He stays away from the celebration because he never forgives. How good the father is! He goes out to find that son too, just as he had run to meet the prodigal younger son. The father invites his self-righteous and lonely son into the place of agreement where forgiveness is. This means that the father himself must bear the alienation of both the younger son and the elder son; such is the mystery behind this petition that Jesus invites us to discover: "forgive us our debts. . . ." Jesus Christ himself is the enormous exception who makes this enormous exception possible.

Additional Notes

The word *aphiemi* is translated in our text by the English word "forgive." It is translated in other places in the New Testament by such words as "abandon," as in Revelation 2:4, and by the words "leave behind," as in John 14:27. It is the word for "divorce" as in 1 Corinthians 7:11. This word, therefore, in the literal sense means to leave behind, to cancel, to abandon; and, therefore, it becomes the word in the New Testament for forgiveness. God leaves behind and cancels our sins.

9

TOTAL HELP FOR
TOTAL NEED

And lead us not into temptation,
But deliver us from evil.

(Matt. 6:13)

The prayer now closes with one final request that might be translated, "Lead us not into perils too great for us to bear, and protect us from the evil one."

Temptation is a fierce and frightening word not only in English but in the language of the Bible too. *Peirao* means to destroy by degrees; it means to place someone under the peril of intense, gradual stress. *Peirao* may in some cases mean "to test" in a positive sense, but it is made all the more frightening in the way it is used in the New Testament when the word's context is not positive, but clearly hostile. There is a devious and deceptive quality that is always contextually attached to the word in such instances.

Temptation and Its Source

The peril of temptation is not the same danger as the peril of a frontal attack by a foe who has openly announced his motives as an adversary. Instead of such an open challenge, temptation is a much more subtle kind of stress. It is the stress that encourages its victims to make their own false moves so that in the end they destroy themselves. It is like the riverbank jumping contest in John Knowels' book *A Separate Peace* in which the older and more athletic boys arrange for younger boys who are not as athletically mature to engage in an initiation jump from a tree. The jump is designed to place a stress on the younger boys beyond their athletic competence. In the end the jump is not therefore a fair contest. It is a temptation because the goal is not to test skill but rather to bring harm to one particular lad who is tempted to jump far beyond any possibility of his skill. He tries to make the jump because of his desire to please persons he mistakenly thinks are his friends.

This is temptation. It looks as if a person who is tempted has destroyed himself or herself, but in fact the person was drawn toward a destructive bad choice by a tempter. Temptation is usually not aimed at physical harm; it is usually designed to produce moral harm, as in the case where one individual asks a question of another person, not in order to hear an answer or an opinion, but to entrap and discredit the one being questioned. The result of such a verbal snare is the same as the high tree in *A Separate Peace;* in both cases the intended victim destroys himself or herself by the response they make to the carefully arranged entrapment because there is a deception at the core of the question.

The only way to know therefore whether *peirao* is used in New Testament texts in the hostile sense of *tempt* or in the positive sense of *test* is to closely observe the motivational context. In both cases the questions may "sound" just about the same. In the one instance the strong and stressful experience is posed to us in order to strengthen our lives as, for example, in the tough conditioning weeks at the opening of football season. In that time the coach deliberately puts his team through a rigorous conditioning period of both physical and emotional hardship. His goal as a coach is not to destroy his players but to toughen them up so they will not become injured or disoriented in the pressures of an actual game. The team is being put under stress to strengthen it.

In the same way Jesus asked his disciples the question about how they would propose to feed the five thousand, not in order to destroy or discredit them, but to strengthen them and heighten their experience of the wondrous solution to the question. It is interesting to me that following that initial question by Jesus in John's narrative of the event he calls the question a test by Jesus. The word *peirao* is used (John 6:6). The disciple Andrew came forward with a suggestion about a boy's lunch and according to John's Gospel, the great crowd was fed miraculously by Jesus' mighty act—but in a way that honored Andrew's suggestion. In the end the disciples are not destroyed by the experience. They are permanently strengthened. Jesus, like a good coach, put his team under a healthy stress to strengthen them.

Temptation is altogether different. The stresses are now used toward the goal of disintegration, to demoralize the targeted person or persons. It may appear on the surface like the rugged stresses of the football coach's conditioning program, but when the motives are revealed it becomes clear that the pressures, whether subtle or blatant, have one goal and that is to destroy. The contest is not fair because of the hidden agenda which is not previously or honestly disclosed. It is not therefore a fair fight or a fair contest because what was put forward as a question for information was really not that at all. The initiation jump was not really intended as an invitation to join the fraternity of friends at all. Temptation therefore according to the Bible is always evil! We are given by James a very clear statement in this connection: "Let no one say when he is tempted, 'I am tempted by God'; for God cannot be tempted with evil and he himself tempts no one" (James 1:13). This means that God does not test us in order to break us, but like the good coach he disciplines us in order to build us up for the endurance we will need so that we may play the game, and last throughout the whole sixty minutes of play.

It is the devil who tempts. In fact he is called "the tempter" in Matthew 4:3. This means that when we humans play out that destructive role toward other human beings or toward any part of God's creation we have taken up the strategy and the way of evil, even the evil one. The "question" that intends to arrange for another human being's self-destruction, the physical "adventure" that lures another person toward harm's way—are both acts of temptation. Regardless of how pure or innocent they may appear on the surface, the fact is they originate in hell, and they will be judged by God for what they are and not how they appear.

This is the evil that is at the core of such events as a bullfight, a cockfight, or a pit bulldog fight. In each case persons under the masquerade of "sport" have created a deceptive setting, a cruel hoax into which these animals are placed in order to be fatally tempted while gamblers and spectators—who are the tempters—watch animals respond in panic. Each of these creatures is a part of God's good creation and we have been entrusted by God to be their stewards. Just as God will indeed judge us for all sin against other human beings, he will also judge us for our sin against the earth and these "games" of terror against the creatures of the earth.

The Temptations of Jesus

Jesus Christ endured the assault of temptation at its most furious intensity. The New Testament describes these as three assaults of temptation by the devil in which our Lord was tempted to distrust the Father and to abandon his own integrity and ministry (Matt. 4, Luke 4). Jesus' adversary used the very language of faith in order to tempt him (Satan quotes from the Messianic Psalm 91 in order to lure Jesus away from the hard pathway of ministry that he had chosen, enticing him instead to take a spectacular leap from the temple roof). But the devil's intention was to guide Jesus toward the place of abandonment of his own freedom and toward a distrust of his Father's faithfulness.

The method and the goal of the tempter's assault upon our Lord gives us our very best insight into the strategy and intention of temptation. Because of this classic temptation we are encouraged to ask the key questions of all tests that are posed to us, from whatever source they come:

- What is the goal of the test or the invitation toward experience?
- Is it to strengthen my life?
- Is it to draw me closer toward my own real self, toward others, and the Lord of life?

In this we have the all-important difference between the ministry of *conviction of the Holy Spirit* and the *temptation of the devil*. If a line of questioning is leading me toward the conclusion that my life is not only sinful but that there is no hope for me before God, then this line of questioning is not the healthy conviction of sin by the Holy Spirit. It is the temptation by the devil by which I am being encouraged to distrust God's love and faithfulness. That is moral temptation! The conviction of sin by the Holy Spirit always leads me toward the Redeemer, always toward hope, whereas despair is the end result of temptation's line of questions.

However, it is also possible for temptation to create a line of reasoning that apparently leads toward the opposite direction. But in the end the same lonely isolation results. I may be tempted toward self-pride, just as I may be tempted toward self-disgust. Though each approach to me is apparently opposite in purpose, nevertheless each is the work of the temptation of evil and both lead toward aloneness, loss of freedom, and distrust of the faithfulness of God. In the one case I don't think I need God because of a false perception of my greatness and in the other I am afraid to need him because I accept the false teaching that because of my sinfulness my life is beyond all possibility of his keeping care.

We Don't Face Temptation Alone

Jesus Christ, the one who endured temptation, is the one who now in his sermon teaches us to pray "lead us not into temptation." The best reading of this sentence is the simplest. It is clear that what Jesus now encourages us to pray is that we be spared from the deceptive stresses that are too great for us to bear. Jesus encourages his disciples to request help from God against the subtle attack of temptation. The prayer is realistic about the existence of such threats and each one of us has stories to tell of the experiences of this peril. But the good news is that we now know that Jesus Christ himself stands with us in the face of the danger of temptation; he has taken hold of temptation and has recognized its threat. But more than that, Jesus has invited his disciples to bring this danger before our Father and seek his help.

The most important thing for us to recognize—and this part of the Our Father Prayer affirms it to us—is that we do not face temptation alone. Temptation which seeks to destroy our freedom by our own bad use of that freedom is possible only because we are free creatures. And we have freedom because of God's decision. Our Lord never robs us of freedom in our discipleship journey, which is one reason that temptation is a real possibility at every point along the way of that discipleship journey.

This parallel request reminds us that the origin of temptation is actually Satan. Yet we are not his pawns. This prayer bears witness to the complex and real freedom that we have. Temptation is our problem because we have the privilege of deciding major questions. A tree is not tempted. A cat is not tempted when a bird is exposed to its leap, because the cat is unaware of the bird's right to life. Only human beings make that kind of decision and, therefore, temptation is our real problem. Jesus invites us to blurt out the cry for help at just such crisis moments as when the peril of temptation is nearby.

"Deliver Us From Evil"

The final sentence of the Lord's Prayer, as found in the most ancient manuscripts of Matthew's text, is the prayer for help against the evil one. The Bible takes seriously the existence not only of evil in the sense of human failure but also in the larger suprahistorical sense portrayed by this phrase. As God in his sovereign wisdom has provided for human freedom, so that we are able to choose against his good will for us, so also in the cosmic order God has allowed a freedom that has resulted in the existence of evil at that level of reality too. That evil is the devil. The whole of the Bible takes the existence of this greater evil with level-headed and complete seriousness.

"From the *evil one (poneroi)*." The word *poneroi* as used in the New Testament refers to evil in a human sense and also evil in a cosmic sense. This prayer not only seeks God's help against our own human forms of evil but it seeks

God's help against cosmic evil too, and at its very source. St. John Chrysostom on this text also recognizes the many dimensions and the complexity of evil. He writes first about the cosmic form of evil and then about the human form of evil. "And Christ here calls the devil 'the wicked one' commanding us to wage against him a war that knows no truce." Later in his commentary he reflects upon evil in its human dimension. "For wickedness is not of those things that are from nature, but of them that are added by our own·choice."

Chrysostom tells us that by this prayer—"deliver us from the evil one"—we signal once and for all that we are engaged as Christians in a battle against all forms of evil, a battle that knows no truce. It is a battle in which we need God's resources because behind all evil at its source is the evil one. This means that there are many different kinds of evil; there are bad choices made by individual human beings, there is also the wider crisis of dehumanization that makes up evil in the social whole, and there is evil at the cosmic level of creation too.

This third level poses a profound mystery. As God in his sovereign wisdom allowed for our human freedom by which we are free to choose for righteousness or against righteousness, so also in the heavenly realm of creation God allowed for a freedom resulting in the possibility of choice against God's will at that level. The Bible, Old and New Testaments, describes evil at the heavenly level of the created order as the devil, the evil one, Satan; if we put together the biblical explanation and descriptive narratives concerning Satan within Scripture we may define the devil as follows: *moral personal will against the will of God at the heavenly level of God's created order.*

The Larger Battle With Evil

From the Bible's point of view we will not have realistically grappled with human evil and all earthly wickedness unless we also grapple with this "will against God's will."

This means that there is a larger battle before us than what we know of as our own struggle against our selfishness and mistakes; evil has a more ominous sting and complexity within its essential nature.

This multidimensional nature of the problem of evil has been recognized not only in the Bible but in all great literature and in particular in folk tales, the ancient myths and fantasy stories of all cultures. Evil is rarely portrayed in such literature as simple or one-dimensional, but is shown as multi-layered. This is true in *Snow White and the Seven Dwarfs, The Wizard of Oz, Grimm's Fairy Tales, The Chronicles of Narnia,* and *The Lord of the Rings.*

For example, in *The Lord of the Rings* by J. R. R. Tolkien, there are many levels of evil, but they reach several crescendos of complexity and intensity. What Frodo must face in his final hours with the ring is a different kind of evil and a different kind of temptation than that which confronts him in the clumsy attacks by the spider-like Gollum. In the same way the wizard Gandalf at the bridge of Khazad-Dûm must face a rage from Balrog that is more total than the dangers faced by his companion travelers. Tolkien has, as a storyteller, recognized in the separate situations throughout the adventure the different kinds of the threats of evil and therefore different kinds of struggle that are encountered by the villians and heroes of the story.

His fantasy story faces these varied kinds of intensity and degree and acts them out in terms of an adventure story with Hobbits and other marvelous imaginary creatures. But as a philosopher, Tolkien, like all great folk story writers, has echoed an awareness about good and evil that all human beings are able to feel and sense in different ways and to different degrees. All great fantasy and folk stories are in one way or another focused around the battle between good and evil. What is important for us to recognize now is that the portrayal of evil is always multi-layered. We will later make the same observation in regard to the portrayal of the reality of good.

The most successful motion pictures of the last decade are three adventure movies by George Lucas which strongly resemble the J. R. R. Tolkien Middle Earth adventures. These movies—*Star Wars, The Empire Strikes Back,* and *Return of the Jedi*—are adventure stories portrayed in a modern, space-technology motif. But as for the essential story line and portrayal of the contest between good and evil these films are very much in the tradition of the folk sagas of Europe, Iceland and ancient Greece. Consider the portrayal of the layered nature of evil that shows up in these three contemporary films:

There is the evil of the faceless soldiers in white who only follow orders, yet their blind obedience leads to harm. They are a blur to us who watch them. Their masks cancel out all individuality and personhood, yet they act efficiently and under discipline—the discipline of evil.

There is the evil of weakness shown in the uncle and aunt of Luke Skywalker who are afraid to take risks for the truth that they know, which truth they have repressed out of fear.

There is the evil of thievery represented by the slave trader thieves who steal the robots and sell them as slaves to the highest bidders. There is the evil of blatant cruelty represented by the sand people who are like the thugs and bullies of every period in human history. There is the evil of chaotic self-indulgence represented in the bizarre café scene. This Sodom and Gomorrah spectacle of luxurious excess and personal chaos is yet another layer in the intricate fabric of evil.

There is the evil of weakness and pride and careless inconsistency represented in both of the heroes of the story, Hans Solo and Luke Skywalker. Because the story is an epic, and therefore a truthful story, the human heroes must also share in the ambiguities and problems of evil themselves.

There is the evil of bureaucratic lust for power represented by the committee that commands the Death Star.

But each of these forms of evil or layers within a highly-complicated whole is dwarfed by a kind of evil that functions at still a stronger and more mysterious level. This is the evil represented by Darth Vader. Here we meet evil that is spiritual and more profoundly complicated than the other forms of evil. Here is evil that once was allied with the Truth, which like an angel of light has fallen away from truth. This form of evil seeks the destruction of what was once an original loyalty.

This evil is more generic than the violence of the sand people or the sexual chaos of the café monsters; this is evil closer to its spiritual source and therefore it is the most dangerous. What is most important is that such malice must be conquered by different weapons than the laser guns of Hans Solo's space ship. Luke must learn of new weapons and of new rules if he is to successfully overpower such evil. The Gandalf figure in Lucas's film epic is Obi-wan Kenobbi, who begins the long process of teaching his young Jedi warrior Luke about the much longer battle that is under way if indeed Darth Vader and his master is to be defeated.

J. R. R. Tolkien, like George Lucas, has portrayed for us in fictional terms the large-scale battle between good and evil. These stories are exciting stories because of the element of adventure that is within them, but they are exciting at another level because they are part of a larger body of folk stories that signal to us that we as human beings worldwide are aware of the continuing contest between good and evil. Not only that, but there is a consciousness of the fact that deeply set within all the different kinds of evil is the spiritual reality of evil as will against the will of ultimate good. These stories bear their own remarkable witness to our awareness of the existence of God and the existence of the devil; our folk stories are one of the most fascinating of all of the proofs of this universal intuition.

The seventeenth-century Puritan Thomas Watson put it very well in his commentary on the Lord's Prayer—"Satan envies man's happiness. To see a clod of dust so near to God, and himself, once a glorious angel, cast out of heavenly paradise, makes him pursue mankind with inveterate hatred."

But the prayer that Jesus teaches now has intervened in our behalf. The devil, and for that matter all forms of evil, have power but they do not have final power. There is a boundary beyond the boundary of their terror, and this prayer recognizes that greater boundary. The evil one has the power to accuse, to slander, to tempt—these are his names in the Bible—but he does not have the power to ultimately destroy. One of his names is Apollyon, which means destroyer, but in the book of Revelation where that name appears it becomes clear that though he calls himself by such a terrible name he does not have the power he claims; beyond all harm that evil can do there is the boundary that belongs to Jesus Christ who is the Lord of redemption and life and who is the final judge. It is Jesus Christ who has the real and the lasting power. From Jesus Christ human beings receive the spiritual weapons to conquer cosmic evil and therefore from the standpoint of the New Testament it is very important that we should not overrate the powers of spiritual evil.

The power of this brief and crystal-clear petition in the Lord's Prayer rests in its ability to set us free from the need to fear the evil one. This is the only sentence we need to make use of in order to exorcise demons and all of the evil charades of our generation. We must in fact beware of any exaggeration of the power of evil. When we find ourselves encouraged to overestimate the power of evil, the direct result of that exaggeration is a shrinkage in our real confidence in the faithfulness and authority of Jesus Christ. What also may result because of this backdoor appreciation of evil is a reduction in our own sense of responsibility for the decisions we make and the acts we do. It is never correct either theologically or practically to say "the devil made me do it." The devil only tempts; we are the ones who decide and act. Therefore we are the ones that must ask for forgiveness and we are the ones who must seek God's help and then thank him for his goodness and faithfulness.

There is a larger battle before us than simply the contest between our own selfishness and the good will of God. Against such evil therefore there must be a warrior who fully understands the total scale of the battle. There is such a warrior, and only one. He who teaches this prayer is the one who must make the prayer possible, and this forms the profoundly Messianic element in the prayer. Jesus Christ, and he alone, will win the battle against the evil one. The cross and the empty grave are the battlefields of that greater warfare. His victory fulfills this prayer. Therefore, our strength in the face of evil is the knowledge that Jesus Christ has the upper hand in that great struggle.

For this reason we do not need to be preoccupied with the evil one or his harassment in our present age. It is God's will that we simply pray this prayer. It is enough.

Additional Notes

The Greek word used in the New Testament and translated into English as the word "temptation" is *peirao*. The root meaning of *peirao* in its classical Greek origins means "to strive with" or "to put to the test"; the word is most commonly used in classical Greek in a hostile sense, which carries the connotation of that which places something or someone under such stress that a break occurs because of the stress.

The word, however, is not always used in this hostile sense. It may be used as a strong word for "experience"; that is, something that is experienced in a stressful way could be described by this word.

It is in this second sense that *peirao* is used by the writer to the Hebrews in Hebrews 11:36. The writer is describing the hardships of the people of faith, and tells us that "others *suffered* mocking and scourging, and even chains and imprisonment" (italics added). In this sentence the RSV translators used the English word "suffered" to translate *peirao*. The word implies in this sentence the hard and stressful experience of the people of faith.

John uses this same word to describe an unforgettable encounter between Jesus and his disciples at the occasion of the feeding of the five thousand. Our Lord asks Philip, "How are we to buy bread so that these people may eat?" Following that question John, as the writer of the Gospel, makes this comment: "This [Jesus] said to *test* him, for he himself knew what he would do" (John 6:6, italics added). Jesus, in posing the question to Philip, has tested him; a stress has been placed upon Philip, but as the context makes clear, the test is not presented in order to break Philip. The RSV is therefore correct by its translation of the word *peirao* in this instance as "test." The experience was stressful for Philip, and a strongly felt experience, but not in any sense was it a destructive temptation.

Another interesting special use of the word is found in Revelation 2:2 where the church at Ephesus is commended because they "have *tested* those who call themselves apostles but are not . . ." (italics added). The word is strong and stresses are obvious in the sense of the word, but once again the RSV translators did not rule in favor of the use of the word "tempt" to translate *peirao* in this instance.

The other uses of the word in the New Testament that are of special interest to us are those where it is translated with the English word *tempt*. One example is the very important sentence from Paul in which the apostle helps us to really understand the meaning of the word *peirao* as temptation.

"No temptation has overtaken you that is not common to man. God is faithful, and he will not let you be tempted beyond your strength, but with the temptation will also provide the way of escape, that you may be able to endure it" (1 Cor. 10:13).

Paul has helped us understand the shades of meaning that accompany this word *peirao* in the way it is used in the New Testament. Temptation places upon us the stress of peril too great for us to bear so that in the end we give way under pressure and are broken.

"And deliver us from evil." Most of the English translations of this text translate *tou ponerou* in a neuter sense by the use of the word *evil*. (Augustine preferred this rendering of the word.) The problem with such a translation, however, is that the two words *tou ponerou* can also be translated in the masculine sense as "the evil one" (Tertullian and Origen rendered the word in this direction). John Calvin and Martin Luther both chose to identify the term *tou ponerou* in an inclusive sense to represent the full sweep of evil in all of its forms, as "all moral wickedness" (see Lenski's discussion in *Interpretation of St. Matthew's Gospel,* p. 263). "There is no necessity of raising a debate on this point, for the meaning remains nearly the same," says Calvin. I think that Luther and Calvin are correct in that larger interpretation, because it is important to realize that evil is more than a one-dimensional reality. At this point, therefore, in the Our Father Prayer we are encouraged by Jesus Christ to pray for deliverance from all forms of evil. That brings us to a very important question which I have discussed already in part: What is evil and what are its various dimensions? What does the word mean in its most basic sense in the Greek language? *Poneros,* the root noun, means in a physical sense "sick, spoiled." It is used in this basic sense in Luke 11:34 ". . . When [your eye] is not *sound,* your body is full of darkness" (italics added). This same sense of the word appears in the parallel passage, Matthew 6:23.

Note also Matthew 7:17: "nor can a *bad* tree bear good fruit" (italics added). The sense of the word in each of these sentences is that of "sick, unhealthy, spoiled, worthless." This word in classical Greek as well as in first-century Greek is used by writers as the word for "wicked, evil, bad" in the ethical sense. With the definite article *the,* it becomes one of the terms in the New Testament used to identify the devil.

Notice these examples. In Matthew 13:19 Jesus tells a parable of seeds that fall on hard soil so that "the evil one comes and snatches away. . . ." Our Lord prays for his disciples in John 17:15, "Keep them from the evil one." Paul tells of the armor for the Christian in Ephesians 6:16 that is able to "quench all the flaming darts of the evil one." John tells of our victory because of Christ so that we "have overcome the evil one" (1 John 2:13). In this text of the Our Father Prayer, Matthew 6:13, the possessive (genitive) is used in the same way as earlier in the Sermon on the Mount where Jesus commands his disciples "Let what you say be simply 'Yes' or 'No'; anything more than this comes from evil" (Matt. 5:37).

10
KINGDOM, POWER, AND GLORY

For thine is the kingdom and the power and the glory, forever. Amen.

(Matt. 6:13)

The final ascription—"For thine is the kingdom and the power and the glory, forever. Amen."—is not found either in the Gospel of Luke or in the most ancient Matthew texts. It is a phrase from a prayer of David recorded in 1 Chronicles 29:10–13. Since the ascription does not appear in the earliest manuscripts we conclude that it was probably added here by early Christians in a reverent attempt to complete the Lord's Prayer, which otherwise ends abruptly.

The prayer, as Jesus first taught it to his disciples, probably stopped without such an ending. The prayer is thus more like an opening door through which we, like Digory in C. S. Lewis's story, may enter and rightly pour out our hearts to the Lord.

There are, however, complicated textual problems with regard to this final sentence in view of the fact that it does appear in several manuscripts, if not in the most ancient ones. Let us consider the lines of interpretation if we follow either of these two possibilities: If we omit the final sentence it means that our Lord has taught a prayer to his disciples that is like a door opening into a larger room. He has by this brief prayer taught his followers how to enter that greater room. Now that we are in the room where our Father is we are able to bring ourselves and our needs and our feelings to the Father. We may blurt them out because we know that he hears and he cares. The Lord's Prayer assures us of that care, and now that we have entered the room where he is we are able to enter into the fellowship of worship, praise, and intercession toward which the Lord's Prayer has pointed the way. This means that Jesus has taught a prayer with which to begin our own intimate relationship with God. This intention is confirmed by the fact that the prayer ends without an ending, not even an Amen!

But what if the final ascription indeed belongs in the text? The textual problem for interpreters lies in the fact that there are ancient manuscripts that contain the sentence, "For thine is the kingdom . . . Amen." It is also true that the second-century document *The Didache* contains this final sentence of praise (*Didache* 8:2). One scholar, W. D. Davies, is convinced that the ascription is genuine and belongs in the text. "It is antecedently unlikely that Matthew and, for that matter, Jesus Himself should finish a prayer without a doxology, expressed or assumed . . . secondly, (according to Pharisee tradition) every benediction had to be responded to with the full doxology . . . 'praised be His name whose glorious Kingdom is forever and ever.' " Therefore, as we can see, the technical issues are complicated; yet on the basis of textual evidence we must face the fact that the final sentence is missing from our most valuable and oldest manuscripts of the New Testament.

If Jesus had presented to his followers a prayer without an ending it is understandable that the early church scribes might seek to fulfill Old Testament tradition and first-century Jewish worship practice and therefore draw together a final doxology for the close of the prayer. In any case, the final sentence is almost identical in theme to David's benediction in 1 Chronicles 29:10–13; see also David's benediction in 1 Chronicles 16:36. Another interesting parallel to this doxology is found in the opening sentences of our Lord's high priestly prayer (John 17).

The Kingdom

The doxology acknowledges three facts about God's character in its great shout of praise. The word *kingdom* is a highly charged word in the first century and Jesus has taken the word into his hands at the very first sentence of the Sermon on the Mount. He tells of those who will "inherit the kingdom." And the nine Beatitudes that introduce the sermon make it clear that a new and deeper definition of kingdom is being revealed. But, because of their confinement to the narrow limitations of tribalism and nationalistic aspiration, the disciples of Jesus will only gradually be able to discover what this word is to finally mean. For Jesus it means kingly reign, relationship between God and human beings. It means God's will and the fellowship of the disciples who seek to know and obey God's will.

The disciples will discover this wide and universal sense of the word *kingdom,* but not immediately. It will take time and a series of surprises. By the time of the first great council of the church at Jerusalem the church will agree that God's kingdom is universally available to all who have faith. At that council the disciples will agree that the kingdom is not a territory, but a people of faith who trust in Jesus Christ. The kingdom of David and David's benediction is then universally applied in this prayer.

The Apostle James quoted the prophets in his speech at the Jerusalem council to confirm the point:

> "After this I will return, and I will rebuild the dwelling of David, which has fallen; . . . that the rest of men may seek the Lord, and all the Gentiles who are called by my name, says the Lord, who has made these things known from of old."
>
> (Acts 15:16, 17)

This is the kingdom of God for which we now praise God. It is the kingly reign that belongs to God and becomes the gift to every believer.

The Power

The prayer also thanks God for his power, his authority. In the New Testament, power is not understood as a force that the believer is able to control or make use of. Rather power for the Christian is our confidence that God has the power. Because Jesus Christ has the authority it means that evil does not have that power, nor does death, nor do angels, nor does the devil. This is the real power of the gospel; it is the assurance of the authority that resides with the Father. We don't tap that power as if it were a power transmission line—rather we are assured of the reign of Jesus Christ and of the fact that history is boundaried by his decision.

But having said this there is a tremendous authority that comes to one who is assured of God's authority. It means that such a person is thereby set free from the false powers and from the panic-like fear in the face of the threats of wrongful power. It is something like the fictional character Lucy in C. S. Lewis's Narnia stories. She is never quite so terrified of the dangers of Narnia once she has met Aslan, the great lion, Son of the Emperor from beyond the sea. She has ridden on Aslan's back and that experience of Aslan's authority has brought everything else into clearer focus. This is the power worth having and it is the power we receive from Jesus Christ once we are assured of his forgiveness and of his victory over death. It is not the power we can use as if it were our possession; nor is it the power that we have over against someone else.

This is the power we need most. And it is a power that does not corrupt those who receive it.

I remember, as if it were last evening, an incident that happened in my life when a very close friend of mine was having a struggle with fear. This lad was in the third grade at the time and was suffering from a wave of fear at the thought of going to school each morning. Fortunately for him, this fearfulness was short-lived; but during the days when it assaulted him, it was a very real and terrifying experience. On this one evening, he felt the wave of fear; and as he was getting ready to go to bed, he told me that he was afraid that he would not be able to go to sleep. We read some fun stories and said prayers, but the fear was still very real and intense. I decided to risk making things even worse and suggested that we try to think of all the things we might be afraid of both at nighttime and at school. I knew that my young friend, like I, had read the wonderful Narnia stories and that he knew about Lucy and Susan's grand ride upon Aslan's back. I said to him, "Let's make believe; let's walk right through all these great dangers that scare us: like dragons and snakes and moving shadows and doors that spring open without warning; but just a minute, before we start our trip let me lift you up and put you on Aslan's back—hold on! I'm going to jump up too."

We began our walk through the dark alleyways of our

fears. I was in the middle of a sentence asking my good friend if there was any particular monster he wanted to take a look at when all I could hear was the deep and good breathing of a boy sound asleep. He had felt the golden mane of the great lion, Son of the Emperor from beyond the Sea; and he was not afraid. He could feel the breathing of this one who "breathes on a very large scale," and now he was safe. Like all children who have loved Lewis's story, this lad knows who Aslan is; and with the help of his lively imagination, he, as a third grader, was putting his weight down upon the strong goodness of God's Son. Now he could say the final words of his nightly prayer with active understanding: "For thine is the kingdom and the power. . . ." Now, what shall I fear.

The Glory

"And the glory." Glory as a word both in the Old Testament and the New Testament has to do with the presence of God. There is the sense of luminosity and spectacle that accompanies the biblical portrayals of glory. We note this in the great encounter between the prophet and the Lord. Isaiah watched in startled wonder and heard the great song to God, " 'Holy, holy, holy is the Lord of hosts; the whole earth is full of his glory' " (Isa. 6:3).

The disciples on the Mount of Transfiguration had the same experience of the mystery and glory of Jesus Christ: ". . . his face shone like the sun. . . ."

John's vision in Revelation 4 and 5 is also a vision of the glory of God the Father and of the Lamb. He hears a great song: " 'Worthy art thou, our Lord and God, to receive glory and honor and power . . .' " (Rev. 4:11). Glory carries within its meanings the sense and recognition of ultimate worth. We sing the *Gloria* when we have discovered the worthiness of God.

Only God deserves a word as large as glory. It is his by right and it is his to share with humanity. When a human being has caught the vision of the disclosure of the character of God by the Lord God himself, then it is that this word *glory* becomes appropriate as the best description that we are able to come up with from our inadequate vocabulary. The word is used this way in the Old and New Testaments. The word signals to us that God deserves our praise! And as God himself draws us into his presence then we also share in that glory in a reflected way. This is the intent of Paul's great affirmation in Romans 8: "and those whom he called he also justified; and those whom he justified he also glorified" (Rom. 8:30). When we experience this decision of God we are experiencing the approval of God toward us, what the apostle calls "the weight of glory." Listen to Lewis as he reflects upon what this weight of glory means for us:

> . . . either glory means to me fame, or it means luminosity . . . the desire for fame appears to me as a competitive passion and therefore of hell rather than heaven. As for the second, who wishes to become a kind of living electric light bulb?
>
> When I began to look into this matter I was shocked to find such different Christians as Milton, Johnson and Thomas Aquinas taking heavenly glory quite frankly in the sense of fame or good report. But not fame conferred by our fellow creatures—fame with God, approval or (I might say) "appreciation" by God. And then, when I had thought it over, I saw that this view was scriptural; nothing can eliminate from the parable in the divine accolade, "Well done, thou good and faithful servant." With that, a good deal of what I had been thinking all my life fell down like a house of cards. I suddenly remembered that nothing is so obvious in a child—not in a conceited child, but in a good child—as its great and undisguised pleasure in being praised.
>
> (C. S. Lewis, *The Weight of Glory*, p. 8)

There is no more vital experience in the life of a human being than to know who the King really is, and to know of his sovereign righteousness, his ultimate worthiness, and then to experience his approval. Can you see how this final doxology in the Lord's Prayer has brought us full circle to the opening four commandments of God at Mount Sinai? We have been brought to the great worship commandments, the commandments that point us toward God and his character. Here in this doxology is the best protection granted to us against idolatry, vanity, polytheism, and meaninglessness. When I know the King for who he is and I know of his authority and his worthiness, I no longer need the idols of Baal nor of the Roman city-gods nor of the twentieth-century no gods.

The doxology has turned our eyes upon the Lord; and in that turning we have fulfilled the vision of the Law and the Prophets.

"Forever, Amen." The prayer's doxology closes with the words of fulfillment and faithfulness. The word *forever* is not employed in its Greek sense of infinity, but in the Hebrew sense of completion, and this is affirmed to us as we hear the companion word "Amen." *Amen* is a word brought directly into Greek from the Hebrew vocabulary. *Amen* in Hebrew means faithfulness; it means foundation in its literal sense; God is the foundation upon which we may rest our trust. He is trustworthy and with that assurance ringing in our ears we close the prayer that Jesus taught.

Additional Notes

The word *Amen,* in its concrete Hebrew definition, means "foundation stone" or "pillar" as, for example, in 2 Kings 18:16. There it is used to describe the doorposts of the temple. Note also Isaiah 22:22, 23, where the word *Amen* is translated "sure peg." The word is used in a double way as in Psalm 41:13, "Amen and Amen." In this instance it means the faithfulness of God followed by the response of our faith. God's faithfulness for our faith. This is probably the intention in our Lord's double use of the word *Amen* at the opening of many of his speeches in the New Testament.

11
ANOTHER VERSION OF THE GOOD LIFE

Do not lay up for yourselves treasures on earth, where moth and rust consume and where thieves break in and steal, but lay up for yourselves treasures in heaven, where neither moth nor rust consumes and where thieves do not break in and steal. For where your treasure is, there will your heart be also.

The eye is the lamp of the body. So, if your eye is sound, your whole body will be full of light; but if your eye is not sound, your whole body will be full of darkness. If then the light in you is darkness, how great is the darkness!

No one can serve two masters; for either he will hate the one and love the other, or he will be devoted to the one and despise the other. You cannot serve God and mammon.

Therefore I tell you, do not be anxious about your life, what you shall eat or what you shall drink, nor about your body, what you shall put on. Is not life more than food, and the body more than clothing? Look at the birds of the air: they neither sow nor reap nor gather into barns, and yet your heavenly Father feeds them. Are you not of more value than they? And which of you by being anxious can add one cubit to his span of life? And why are you anxious about clothing? Consider the lilies of the field, how they grow; they neither toil nor spin; yet I tell you, even Solomon in all his glory was not arrayed like one of these. But if God so clothes the grass of the field, which today is alive and tomorrow is thrown into the oven, will he not much more clothe you, O men of little faith? Therefore do not be anxious, saying, "What shall we eat?" or "What shall we drink?" or "What shall we wear?" For the Gentiles seek all these things; and your heavenly Father knows that you need them all. But seek first his kingdom and his righteousness, and all these things shall be yours as well.

Therefore do not be anxious about tomorrow, for tomorrow will be anxious for itself. Let the day's own trouble be sufficient for the day.

(Matt. 6:19–34)

> Never be ashamed of the name of Jesus Christ, or of his gospel.
> . . . It is the only new thing in the world; all else is as old
> as the hills, even the latest vaccine, and the latest bomb. Only
> the eternal, only that which is the same yesterday, today, and
> forever is really new. Aim, therefore, always at that which is
> at once eternal, universal, personal, concrete.
>
> *—Charles Malik*
> *Princeton Seminary commencement address, 1955*

Jesus now sketches a series of brief illustrations and sayings
that contrast the durability and eternal reality of God's will
with various false options for life. In one sense, Jesus here
expands what was first presented in the Beatitudes as hunger and thirst for righteousness, and as purity of heart.
He again shows his listeners that he is aware of the less-
than-ideal setting in which we live our daily lives, where
false but attractive proposals wait at every turn.

Jesus' literary form of teaching is identical to the kind
of writing we find in the book of Proverbs. He teaches
here in the style of the Old Testament wisdom literature—
epigrams, succinct sayings, images out of daily life, and
vivid stories with one or two major thoughts drawn out
as a teaching conclusion. The rabbis often used such epigrams to trigger more complete thoughts or else to conclude
discussions. Some scholars have even suggested that the
whole of Matthew 5–7 is in literary terms a collection of
the brief, summary epigrams from longer, more detailed
dialogue.

Jesus closes this section with a return to the *daily* empha-
sis we found earlier in his model prayer. Purity of heart
must focus upon the concrete world where I am actually
living the 24-hour cycle alongside every other person. Discipleship is not a fanciful escape into future Kingdom grandeur; it is grappling with the present 24-hour day where
everyone else also must live.

These sayings should caution interpreters from moving
the Sermon on the Mount away from the present tense

to a future dispensation or Kingdom Age. Jesus is clear that these mandates are meant to interfere and interface with the present age. He puts his sayings into a current setting and it is not possible for us to separate them from the real world of here and now.

The result may be awkward and difficult but all the more meaningful because of that very incongruity. What we have in the Sermon on the Mount is the breakthrough of God's will for human life into our time frame. God's will does not fit comfortably into our categories; it stands alongside and over against them in judgment, yet also in hope because Jesus' words call us to a new way.

Collision Points

"Where your treasure is, there will your heart be also."

The text reads literally, "do not treasure treasures on earth where moth and rust. . . ." The double use of the word *thesauros* is used and there is poetic power in this unusual double use of the word. We are told not to treasure treasures. In other words, the concrete treasures of our daily lives must have a greater source of durability than that which they have within their own nature.

Jesus recognizes that, as human beings, we are the treasurers who seek out that which we may honor and highly prize. We notice that Jesus does not reject this treasuring instinct which begins very early in our lives and continues throughout our life journey. Our problems with the treasuring instinct begin when we become confused and the instinct is exploited by selfishness and the temptation to idolatry so that we treasure the temporary wasting asset and attach more importance to certain treasures than they deserve. The result of such confusion is that we cease to enjoy and steward the bountiful treasures of God's creation for what they really are: temporary and good gifts presented to us during the journey of our lives. This is the confusion of idolatry; it is idolatry that seeks to freeze and possess the temporary good gifts of creation as if they could be permanent markers and proofs of our worth. We give our hearts to them in the search for enduring worth; and in return, they can give us only what they really are, and that is a wasting treasure. But even that is now destroyed, because it has been misused and misunderstood. In the end, we lose our affection and our hope in the disappointment of the treasure that fades away in front of our eyes like a desert mirage. It happened because our affection and hope had been misplaced in the first place.

The word translated in our text as "moth" is literally the Greek word *brosis,* which means "eating" (as in 1 Corinthians 8:4). It is the word used by the Septuagint translators of the Old Testament when they translated the Hebrew word *insect,* at the larva stage, as in Malachi 3:11. What a powerfully accurate parable Jesus has given us in this larva image. The treasures of the world, when they are wrongly glorified and worshiped, are like the wool sweater with the larvae of the moth hidden up the sleeve. Sooner or later, we will know that it was there all along.

But Jesus does not intend to simply warn his listeners of the dangers of the heart's affection misplaced. He also teaches positively about the meaning and possibility of a healthy perspective: "The eye is the lamp of the body. So, if your eye is sound. . . ." The Greek word here translated "sound" is the word *haplous.* This word means literally "single," "sound," "generous," "sincere." It is the word used in Luke 11:34 where it is also translated as "sound"—the sound eye is the opposite of the evil eye of the selfish laborers in our Lord's parable of the laborers in which Jesus tells of the owner who answers those who have complained of his paying such high wages to the eleventh-hour workers: "Do you begrudge my generosity?" What an exciting word. "Do you begrudge me my goodness (*agathos*)?" This helps us to catch something of both the healthy warmth as well as the sovereignty of the word. The master is so healthy and inwardly resolved that he is able to set a fair and generous wage without the grudging and narrow advice of the all-day workers. In other words, healthiness is seen as the perspective of a person who is not dominated or coerced by the various forces that surround him. The same word (*haplous*) is used in James 1:5 and is there translated "generous."

It is clear that in these sentences Jesus is continuing to present his commentary on the Law of Moses. What we have here is our Lord's teaching on the commandment, "Thou shalt not covet."

But Jesus has not only warned us against the dangers of coveting. He has also presented to us a very important insight into the psychology of coveting (treasuring) and into the philosophical significance of treasures. He follows this with his teaching on clear vision as the secret to the healthy way. We need to see the world around us in the right way, in a healthy way. This is the grand, positive theme that fulfills the Tenth Commandment, "Thou shalt not covet."

God's will for us is not negative but positive: We will see the world in a generous and healthy way, not in a grasping and desperately clutching way. In the deepest sense, what Jesus does is to urge his listeners to see the world from God's perspective so that we discover our own personal worth from God himself; and not only that, but also the worth and meaning of every earthly treasure from God's perspective. When this happens, we are set free from the various despairing results of the attachment of our lives to anything other than the true author of our existence— God himself.

Jesus is teaching in these epigrams that we are to derive the meaning of our lives from God's decision about the earth rather than from the earth itself. Paul offers his own statement of this perspective in his famous sentences: "Do not be conformed to this world, but be transformed by the renewal of your mind, that you may prove what is the will of God, what is good and acceptable and perfect" (Rom. 12:2). Our human worth, therefore, is endorsed by the gospel and not by the accidents of our success or failure with the creation. Everything in the creation rusts in its own way, but God's Word remains.

Do we see in these practical illustrations how Jesus has taught the implications of "thy kingdom come" (v. 10)? The result of this Kingdom way of looking at life does not mean that I become careless and casual about my stewardship of creation. (Jesus will later in this sermon make our practical stewardship mandate clear.) Rather, I will not ask of earthly things that which they cannot give to me. They cannot impart meaning, hope, love, faith, or relationship. They need worth and meaning granted to them from a greater source.

I am convinced that we human beings function best in our relation to houses, lands, and other economic treasures when we see that these parts are indeed parts of a larger whole; and in that wholeness, they gain their meaning from Jesus Christ. I am a better engineer if I do not belong to Boeing or IBM, but rather see engineering as a part of the larger stewardship obligation toward the earth that God has decided and mandated for the good of creation. I am even better as an engineer at Boeing when I do not cling too tightly and ask too much from my stewardship mandate.

This principle is true in every stewardship task of the Christian disciple. We are better mothers, fathers, husbands, sons, and daughters when these relationships are seen in the larger context of God's love and purpose for life. We own possessions such as homes and cars and clothes and cameras in a more wholesome way when we do not own them too much.

Additional Notes

Jesus teaches in the Old Testament tradition just as we find in the book of Proverbs. The verses in this section offer some excellent examples of this kind of wisdom teaching. Note the use of briefly stated images, followed by a simply stated implication. Compare these verses to Proverbs 2 and 3. Jesus makes use of all of the literary forms found in Proverbs. There is the use of short story (7:9–11), analogy (6:22), irony (6:34), direct moral advice (6:23), hypothetical question (6:28), argument of consequences (6:19), statement of logical observation (6:21), and parallel restatement (6:24).

12
WHO GETS THE LAST WORD?

Judge not, that you be not judged. For with the judgment you pronounce you will be judged, and the measure you give will be the measure you get. Why do you see the speck that is in your brother's eye, but do not notice the log that is in your own eye? Or how can you say to your brother, "Let me take the speck out of your eye," when there is the log in your own eye? You hypocrite, first take the log out of your own eye, and then you will see clearly to take the speck out of your brother's eye.

Do not give dogs what is holy, and do not throw your pearls before swine, lest they trample them under foot and turn to attack you.

(Matt. 7:1–6)

The root idea of the Greek word translated "judge" in this passage is "to sunder, to part, to sift, to divide out." Once again in the Sermon on the Mount, Jesus gives a set of mandates that contrast with each other. We are told in 7:1 not to "judge" and yet some five verses later we are instructed not to "give dogs what is sacred. . . ." This second counsel requires some form of judgment or decision: Who or what is a "dog" and who or what isn't? What is Jesus teaching?

As with many biblical words, the word *judge* can be used with several different shades and meanings. One can "judge" by being censorious, carping, condemning; in short, judgmental. Or on the other hand, by a judgment one can form an opinion, decide, arrive at an accurate verdict. In this passage it is the first, destructive judging that Jesus prohibits.

Furthermore, "do not judge" tells us that the right to say the last word about our neighbor has been denied us. The Parable of the Speck and the Log teaches that when seeking to judge the neighbor, our own frailty is intensified. And there is even more. The manner in which Jesus intensified the Law earlier, in chapter 5, leaves us little prospect of not finding a speck in our brother's eye, or a log in our own.

Jesus is thereby teaching that we are not God and we never will be. Only God is able to judge perfectly, because he alone is God, the judge of all the earth. Jesus stands firmly with Moses and the Ten Commandments on this issue and opposes many of the religions and philosophical expectations of his time. Egyptians believed that men and women could become divine. Greek philosophers felt that a spark of the divine nature was hidden within the human soul-spirit. Even the secular, pragmatic Romans officially practiced emperor worship on three occasions during the first century. Jesus breaks with each of those expectations. The right to sift and determine the true weight of every life and every part of existence is in the final sense God's right and his alone.

What does that mean for us today?

Four Implications

1. We do not have the last word about *other people,* because our eyes are not clear enough of distortion to really see the true distinctions. "The dividing line is hidden from us," said Karl Barth. This limitation has altogether wholesome results.

One of the most devastating marks of many quasi-Christian cultic movements is the absoluteness of their leaders at just this point. On the basis of dramatic signs, or because of the power of their personalities, these leaders sift and decide without any check or balance either from the biblical witness or from the larger Christian fellowship. They come too quickly to too many conclusions.

Jesus has raised a vital criterion for the evaluation of any disciple, leader or not. Are we humble enough to realize that we too will be judged (7:12)? This is a very important test for the church leader as well as for the follower.

2. We do not have the last word about *doctrines.* Because of what Jesus has taught us in this sermon, we now know that all doctrine is also subject to tests. First of all, does the doctrine align with God's self-disclosure of his character? Both the Old and New Testaments point to the reign of God's self-revelation, Jesus Christ. All doctrines, judgments, teaching, and all sifting of ideas must be subject to God and his revelation. This is the importance of the testing of all doctrine by the appeal to Scripture. All doctrine must be under the text.

Second, our doctrines must always properly begin, as does the Apostles' Creed, with "I believe," not "This is the last word." Only Jesus Christ possesses that final authoritative mark of perfection. Our convictions are not absolute even though they are very important. They show our journey thus far, but our journey is not absolute at any place along its pathway. Only God himself is absolute and never is our faith or our love or our hope absolute.

This does not mean that we cannot think or weigh or work through the meanings and values of doctrine. We must continuously weigh the truths and values that confront us, and all the more carefully since we are well aware of the logs and specks that we must always negotiate. One reason why the study of dogmatics is so important is that the proclamation of the Christian church is always in danger of going astray precisely because of the problem of specks and logs. Therefore, we Christians must always be in the business of testing truth and watching carefully that we do not carelessly throw away the greatest truth so that it is trampled underfoot. We now see that this strange combination of advice given by Jesus does indeed fit together. We must keep a healthy restraint upon our judgments because of our self-awareness of our own imperfections; and at the same time because of these self tendencies of ours to misread the text due to specks and logs, we must all the more be careful to evaluate every religious and political and personal doctrine that claims our affection and our loyalty so that we do not sacrifice the greater truth of the gospel of God for some particular lesser truth that does not deserve our loyalty.

3. We do not have the last word about *history.* We are now better able to understand our Lord's counsel, "Do not be anxious about tomorrow" (6:34) and also, "which of you by being anxious can add one cubit to his span of life?" (6:27). History past, present, and future belongs to the decision of God; we are to live creatively within history, but we are not its final arbiters. This limitation protects against the arrogance and cynicism that always results when human beings lose their modesty about the journey they share with the rest of the created order. The modesty that Jesus' commandment places upon us will not adversely affect our missionary mandate to be cross-cultural and world Christians who share our faith worldwide. In fact, the air is cleared for us to share all the more enthusiastically when

we know what exactly it is that we have to share with the world. We do not have a theory of our own about history to share; we do not have our own socioreligious movement to share. Each of these can be arrogant, socialized projections of our own value systems and our own journey experiences now made normative for others. We share "not ourselves, but Jesus Christ as Lord, with ourselves as your servants for Jesus' sake," said St. Paul. What we have to share is *extra nos;* it is outside ourselves and this means that it has its own inner integrity and cross-cultural relevance because of the universal center of that gospel who is Jesus Christ himself. The fact is that the best missionaries have been the culturally and historically modest ones who were, therefore, all the bolder about the Lord who did not belong to them as their cultural possession, but whom they knew as their possessor.

4. We do not have the last word about *ourselves.* God alone has that right, and the result for us is the wonderful freedom to be mere Christians and neither gods or demigods. It is God's will that we should live our lives under his will; we are not to do more than that, or less. When we are aware of this good limitation, then we can preserve the dignity of holy things (v. 6) without the danger of fanaticism, or the arrogance of placing too much responsibility on our own shoulders. It is God's decision that he and he alone measures our growth and our fulfillment of his will.

I remember talking to a deeply depressed person who told me a tragic story of personal and interpersonal failure. Not once did he blame anyone else for his downward spiral. He was completely to blame according to the terms of his account. He concluded with a cynical write-off of his own worth.

I asked him to read a Scripture aloud and to give me his impression of what it meant. I handed him Matthew 7:1–6, and he read it aloud. I then asked, "Do you have the right to say the last word about yourself any more than you do about anyone else?" He began to see the liberation of good news in this warning of Jesus. It was like a splash of cold water—good, brisk, and clarifying.

God is our Redeemer and Lord. He is the Judge and we are not. Paradoxically, as we learn to make a "right judgment" (John 7:24), we become more and more obedient to the Supreme Judge, who alone has the last word.

By this great mandate Jesus has called us back from the way of pride and judgmentalism. His kindness has imposed a limitation that is for our benefit. The way of pride inevitably becomes the way of despair because sooner or later the grand claims we make for ourselves will turn toward us an accusing finger of self-judgment. He has a better will for our lives.

Preserving Pearls

Jesus now adds a comment about discernment in sharing. He teaches that we are to be strategic in our witness to the grace of the gospel. In the world where we live we are to find the right time to speak; we are to be prophetic listeners and thoughtful advocates as well as prophetic speakers. Paul's advisers at Ephesus were correct in counseling the apostle to keep silent during the chaotic fury of the crowd at the amphitheater where the people shouted for two hours; Luke shows us (Acts 19) that that was not the time or place for a word from the gospel. Thus Paul did not toss his pearls before swine. A hysterical crowd was trampling down every new idea or possibility. Therefore, Paul must wait for a better moment to speak.

It is not that the people gathered that day at the great Ephesian theater were in fact swine, because they were not. But the chaotic situation was hysterical; in such a setting people are like herds of animals that panic at a provocation and trample down anything that stands in the way. Horrible injustices have been done by ordinary human beings who were herded toward evil acts because of intense fear or anger. Singly they would never have become a party to lynchings and street violence had not a climate of chaos or hostility been aroused in them. At such moments the one person who has perspective and a higher loyalty to justice and the way of righteousness must have an interim strategy to buy enough time for a calming of the intensity level so that the positive, healing word of the gospel may have its moment at the right time and in the right place. A person who is stoned with drugs or drunk with alcohol needs several interim things to happen—such as coffee, food, a night's sleep, perhaps time in jail—before it is either appropriate or right to talk about the meaning of life and life's grand design.

This does not mean that the gospel is not powerful, but rather that it is so true and deep that it deserves a serious hearing. Jesus often put the same point this way: "He who has ears to hear, let him hear."

Additional Notes

A uniquely dangerous element in judgment, as a human exercise, comes into focus in the letter to the church at Ephesus, quoted in the book of Revelation (2:1–7). These Christians at Ephesus were able to discern false prophets; but within their own character a hardening had taken place which required the Holy Spirit to accuse them of abandoning "the love [you] had at first" (v. 4). Their zeal at tracking down those who were false teachers had caused them to become self-righteous and brittle. Ironically in just such a state they were accused by the Holy Spirit of discarding the greatest truth before the swine of their own self-righteousness.

Paul showed the same concern for the church in Corinth; the people were perhaps too zealous in their discipline of a wayward member of the church (2 Cor. 2:5–11). "I beg you to reaffirm your love for him," Paul said. The problem with judgment is that we enjoy it too much. And it often covers our own need of God's grace, hence these warnings in the New Testament letters are very important and contemporary.

13
AN OPEN DOOR POLICY

Ask, and it will be given you; seek, and you will find; knock, and it will be opened to you. For every one who asks receives, and he who seeks finds, and to him who knocks it will be opened. Or what man of you, if his son asks him for bread, will give him a stone? Or if he asks for a fish, will give him a serpent? If you then, who are evil, know how to give good gifts to your children, how much more will your Father who is in heaven give good things to those who ask him. So whatever you wish that men would do to you, do so to them; for this is the law and the prophets.

(Matt. 7:7–12)

First, a promise, and then a story: "Ask, and it will be given you; seek . . . knock. . . ." Jesus has brought us back to the note of joy with which his sermon began. The promise is uncomplicated. We hear no special procedures or religious rituals that must be observed in order for us to qualify. Jesus simply invites those who mourn, who are thirsty, who are poor to bring their needs with them. The credential we need is strangely enough our need itself, and our decision to ask for God's help.

These simple promises are of very important theological significance to this total document we call the Sermon on the Mount. The words of Jesus up to this point have created as many problems for his hearers (and readers) as they have resolved. We now know the grand purposes of the Law which it has been our Lord's intention to explain; but if the Law was hard to follow when we read it before, it is even harder now. Jesus has intensified the Law's purpose by drawing the great arc of the Law around to its fulfillment.

But this clarification, though wonderfully good, is also impossibly hard. Who can do it? Jesus has preserved our humanity in his denial of our right to say the last word about either the neighbor or ourselves. But now the very large question is this: Is Jesus aware of the crisis his words have caused? I believe that he is and that this whimsically simple set of promises with the parable about a father and his son have made it clear that the gospel is in the sermon just as the fulfillment of the Law is in the sermon.

Jesus invites us to come to him for help. "It is good to be weary and worn out in the vain pursuit of the true good so that we may open our arms to the Redeemer" (Pascal). Jesus does not describe how these offers of help will be subsequently won for us by his own act of sacrifice at the cross and victory over the grave, because these are truths that can only be understood by the disciples as they become events. Now, he only invites us to come, and to leave the task of resolution in his hands.

Following this invitation, Jesus takes up the larger question. What kind of God will we find when we dare to seek him? The story of the son requesting bread from his earthly father tells us that God is good, and his will for creation is good. God does not play deceptive games with those who approach him; he does not give a serpent to those who ask for a fish. At the heart of God's relationship with humanity is integrity and earnestness. The friendly earnestness we observe in Jesus Christ throughout his ministry is the essence of the Father's character as well.

Earlier I referred to *The Magician's Nephew* by C. S. Lewis, and the scene in which Digory blurts out his deep anxiety to the great lion, Aslan. The next few sentences in that encounter are very moving. Up to that point, Digory has been looking down at the great claws of Aslan. There is the sense here of the awesomeness and truth of God, with whom we have to deal. Aslan makes no answer to Digory's appeal for help for his mother, but as the boy speaks his heart, he looks up at the face of the lion—and in Aslan's eye he sees a tear. Instantly Digory knows that Aslan loves his mother as much as he does. It is this event discovery that resolves his deepest questions and not words about possible cures.

We are at the place in this unforgettable sermon where Jesus Christ has invited us into his house. We may bring our real selves to this encounter. No games will be played with our feelings or our lives. There will be surprises in the way of discipleship, not of humiliation or betrayal, but they will be surprises of joy. In the gospel we discover that "the serious business of heaven is joy," as Chesterton said.

This is the great "whosoever" part of the Sermon on the Mount. "Every one who asks receives. . . ." These verbs—"ask," "seek," and "knock"—are freedom words. They are not only the invitation to a party but also the call to a decision. The good news is that these invitation words are universally offered.

Throughout the New Testament, salvation is always portrayed in freedom terms. For example, the word *redemption*, which is one of the most important salvation words in the New Testament, means literally "to set free." The more we grow in our relationship with Jesus Christ, the more freedom and obligation we experience—freedom from the power of sin, death, and the devil; freedom toward the way of righteousness and life. But freedom means that we have decisions to make; therefore the invitations to "seek" require of us a decision in our favor.

We never lose our freedom to err, to make bad choices, to go against the will of God. It was always a faulty doctrine of sanctification that taught that as the Holy Spirit fully assures us of Christ we somehow, through the power of the Holy Spirit, rise above this freedom. Ours is not only a good-way freedom; by God's decision we also retain the right to use our freedom badly. Therefore we never outgrow the Lord's Prayer with its petition, "Lead us not into temptation."

So we are called to decide, to do, and to be. What will we ask of our Father? The final teachings of this sermon will explore the wide implications of this freedom theology.

A Golden Rule

"So whatever you wish that men would do to you, do so to them; for this is the law and the prophets." This good sentence of ethical implication follows naturally from the good promise that assures us of the love of God toward us who reach out for help. In the New Testament, we have an ethic of fulfillment, and this is precisely the language that Jesus uses here in this place to describe that ethic: "for this is the law and the prophets." We love because we have been first loved, and it is this evangelical ethic that grants the inner truth, force, and power to the Golden Rule. We are not commanded to love as if love were our resource that we could give to others; instead, we receive God's prior love and forgiveness, and from that fulness we experience the love that compels us to reach out in sharing.

Jesus has now shown that the ethical commands (the second tablet of the Ten Commandments) are not technical prescriptions about what constitute adultery or murder or robbery. Rather, they point toward the grand design of the Law which is, in its deepest sense, care for the well-being of the neighbor just as we have been cared for by God. As we ourselves desire to be cared for and loved, we now know that this universal longing we share with all human beings is the very mandate Christ has granted to us.

Additional Notes

Jesus' invitation and parable has its Old Testament precedent in the promise of Isaiah 65, "Before they call I will answer, while they are yet speaking I will hear" (v. 24).

The "Golden Rule" epigram in verse 12 appears also in Luke 6:31. Note a similar statement in Matthew 22:39, 40, where Jesus quotes Leviticus 19:18. See also Romans 13:9, Galatians 5:14, and James 2:8.

14
THE NARROW PASS

Enter by the narrow gate; for the gate is wide and the way is easy, that leads to destruction, and those who enter by it are many. For the gate is narrow and the way is hard, that leads to life, and those who find it are few.

Beware of false prophets, who come to you in sheep's clothing but inwardly are ravenous wolves. You will know them by their fruits. Are grapes gathered from thorns, or figs from thistles? So, every sound tree bears good fruit, but the bad tree bears evil fruit. A sound tree cannot bear evil fruit, nor can a bad tree bear good fruit. Every tree that does not bear good fruit is cut down and thrown into the fire. Thus you will know them by their fruits.

Not every one who says to me, "Lord, Lord," shall enter the kingdom of heaven, but he who does the will of my Father who is in heaven. On that day many will say to me, "Lord, Lord, did we not prophesy in your name, and cast out demons in your name, and do many mighty works in your name?" And then will I declare to them, "I never knew you; depart from me, you evildoers."

(Matt. 7:13–23)

The freedom words of Jesus—"ask," "seek," and "knock"—
now call upon those who hear them to choose the way
of costly grace. Dietrich Bonhoeffer, the German theologian
who died in the Flossenburg camp on April 9, 1945, wrote
a very significant twentieth-century commentary on the
Sermon on the Mount. It forms Part Two of his book *The
Cost of Discipleship*. In it he puts the crisis of Jesus' words
into stark relief: "The path of discipleship is narrow, and
it is fatally easy to miss one's way and stray from the path,
even after years of discipleship." [1] Jesus challenges his listeners to choose to follow *his* way, though it is narrow,
rather than choose false ways that may be more accessible
and easier to find.

These roadway sentences have almost the same effect
upon us as the parable Jesus told of the camel and the
eye of the needle (see Matthew 19:23–26). His disciples
object to that parable with an obvious reaction, "Who then
can be saved?" Jesus' response to that objection is not pessimistic and narrow, but generous and totally surprising:
"With men it is impossible, but with God all things are
possible."

At this point in the Sermon on the Mount, Jesus makes
use of the roadway language of the Torah to preserve for
us the basic fact that truth is narrow and focused and is
not vaguely generalized. A football game must be played
during sixty exact minutes, and each of these minutes is
carefully timed. This means that there is a precise, "narrow"
restriction that enables the game to be played. Without
this strict time restriction, the game as a sports event would
be meaningless. It would be much easier to eliminate 30-
second clocks and time-out rules toward a more casual concept of play. But such a broad-way interpretation would
destroy the very element that makes the final minutes before
the end of the first half, and the final minutes before the
end of the game so exciting both for serious players and
fans. The narrow gate does not reduce the meaning; it instead enhances the meaning.

And this principle that is so important in every game is

also a vital principle for life. It is the serious, narrow-way commitment of two people in love that grants the romance to two people in love. This is why *Romeo and Juliet* by William Shakespeare is a more compelling and romantic story than *Couples* by John Updike. The one story is of two people in love against heavy odds, whereas the second is the story of almost every consenting adult in a New England town sleeping with another at one time or another without either guilt or joy. The people in the one story are memorable because of the imprint of definite, unforgettable character, whereas those in the second story are blurred together as modern affluents terribly bored and boring; they have nervous reactions but very little soul. It is a rule in literature that without the existence of a "narrow pass"—without the presence of the sense of a line of truth and the reality check that goes with that line of truth—there is very little real romance or real tragedy or real comedy.

Therefore, when Jesus calls the human family to seek the narrow pass of God's will for life, he has on the one hand called each of us to a narrow and hard pathway. But he has also called us to the best way.

This call inevitably confounds and even confuses us because of our own real inadequacy, and it results in our loss of innocence. The Lord of the Sermon has one more time in the sermon brought us back to the promises with which his sermon began. We now feel our poverty more deeply than ever before. We now mourn at a deeper level; and with added realism, we reach out to God for his help.

How shall we know the true pathway from the false? Jesus presents the criterion in parabolic form: "You will know them by their fruits." The tree that has its roots in the will of God does not produce fruit contrary to his character.

The way of righteousness has been disclosed by Jesus Christ within this very sermon. And it is also validated by the way Jesus completes the Law and shows us its grand intent in his own life. We are privileged to see into the deep intention of God's will for the world through the words and acts of Jesus Christ. Therefore we have in that true center, in Jesus Christ himself, the criterion for knowing the difference between the gospel and false gospels.

"Cheap grace is the deadly enemy of our Church. We are fighting today for costly grace. . . . Cheap grace means grace as a doctrine, a principle, a system. . . . the justification of sin without the justification of the sinner. . . . forgiveness without requiring repentance. . . . Cheap grace is grace without discipleship, grace without the cross, grace without Jesus Christ, living and incarnate." [2] Bonhoeffer has given us some examples for testing a false gospel on the basis of its fruits. Or, to put it theologically, *Christology is the crucial turning point in the search for truth.* Who Jesus Christ is and what his Lordship means is the central question of all possible questions—all of the theological questions and all of the ethical ones too! John tells us in his first letter that every spirit (wind) is tested by its relationship to Jesus Christ and its witness to Christ (1 John 4, 5). The false way becomes false primarily when it strays from the true Center who is the person Jesus Christ himself.

Ends vs. Means

Verses 21–25 are introspective and overwhelming: "Not everyone who says to me, 'Lord, Lord,' . . .

In this paragraph Jesus enters the practical debate about ends and means. Do ends justify means? This question has haunted every social and religious movement throughout history. It also confronts each person as he or she sets out a course of ambitious plans for life. Jesus' answer is clear; he teaches that ends and means cannot be separated. A scheme for social and religious good that does not obey God's revealed truth in its daily steps is a false way.

" 'Not every one who *says* to me, "Lord, Lord," . . . but he who does . . .' " (italics added). It is not enough to name the lofty goal because the real test, according to Jesus, is what happens in the journey toward that goal.

We know from personal experiences how realistic and valid this principle is in such human institutions as the family and the church. Parents have goals for their families that may be morally, spiritually, and culturally sound, but the experience of families is that most of the actual values that make up any larger goal are communicated to the family in the routine smaller moments of ordinary daily living under the same roof, more than in the grand design statements about those goals. It is the practical day-to-day values lived out that leave the greater mark upon a child growing up. It is the drive to school, the rainy day at home, the duties of an ordinary twenty-four hour cycle in which we catch from one another the real values by which we live and make decisions. A church is supposed to have great statements of faith but a close look at the church's budget will show up the priorities in the fellowship and its prophetic concerns with more accuracy than do the statements of vision that are published for the Annual Report.

In 1943 Bonhoeffer wrote, "I remember from my student days a discussion between Holl and Harnack as to whether the great historical intellectual and spiritual movements made headway through their primary or their secondary motives. At the time I thought Holl was right in maintaining the former; now I think he was wrong." [3] The secondary motives, goals, and methods are the *means,* and in any movement they last longest, because they represent what the movement is actually *doing* in its daily experience. Regardless of the loftiness of stated objectives, the single steps, which seem so small, are in reality the truest test of the integrity and real goals of a movement. What we actually do in the day-to-day journey is the best clue to the destination that lies ahead. Practical obedience to the way of the gospel, as shown in our secondary methods, is more important than elaborate statements about the kingdom or about heroic love for the masses. Jesus clearly taught that a Christian must even do Christian work Christianly.

There are many practical implications of this teaching, and we might be tempted to complain that such restraints put us as disciples of Jesus Christ at an unfair disadvantage in the world we live in, with its hidden agendas and double-edged protocols. In a sense, this is true; there is a certain swiftness and power that accrues to all movements or ethical systems that reject the unity of ends and means that Jesus here demands. They have the advantage of movable standards, and they are enabled to adopt the ethics of convenience and desire. But a time bomb ticks within such styles of life, whether practiced by a businessman, a labor chief, a religious leader, or a government official. Sooner or later the shortcut will demand its payment.

Jesus himself is our example of integrity between his words and his actions, between means and ends. What Jesus said, he also did. It is, therefore, a distortion of the gospel to pose a theological separation between the timeless ideas of Christ and the Man Jesus who lived among us. His redemption is not only the word of forgiveness spoken to us; it is forgiveness won for us by the work of Jesus Christ himself. "He came and preached peace . . ." says Paul in Ephesians 2:17; he also "[made] peace . . . through the cross" (Eph. 2:15, 16).

"When God decided to break into history with his own character, when he decided to share his love with the world, he decided to do it in personal, not ideological, terms. He came to us as Word in Flesh, Jesus Christ. Jesus Christ is the love of God breaking through and finding us where we really are." [4]

The same unity of word and event is his intention for his disciples. The narrow road of being a Christian forces us to merge *word* and *act*. " 'Not every one who says . . . shall enter the kingdom of heaven, but he who does. . . .' " We are those who must think and speak. But the narrow pass calls us to be and to do as well as to think and say.

Additional Notes

There is a dualism in the New Testament, but it is unlike that which dominates Greek thought and, later, the Gnostic movements. Whereas the Greek dualism is a division between the superior, spiritual order and the inferior, physical order in Jewish and New Testament thought, this dualism is a battle waged between good and evil, within the ethical, spiritual decisions that are made by real human beings and which affect every part of our human existence. I agree with A. M. Hunter that this vital distinction prevails in all of the Gospels of the New Testament, including John's Gospel. "The dualism which pervades the Johannie writings is of precisely the same kind as we discover in the Dead Sea Scrolls, not physical or substantial as in the Greek gnostics, but monotheistic, ethical, eschatological." [5] It is this sort of ethical dualism, with the struggle for truth versus the temptations against truth, that we discover in the "narrow pass" reading of the Sermon on the Mount.

15
BUILDING FOR TOMORROW

Every one then who hears these words of mine and does them will be like a wise man who built his house upon the rock; and the rain fell, and the floods came, and the winds blew and beat upon that house, but it did not fall, because it had been founded on the rock. And every one who hears these words of mine and does not do them will be like a foolish man who built his house upon the sand; and the rain fell, and the floods came, and the winds blew and beat against that house, and it fell; and great was the fall of it.

And when Jesus finished these sayings, the crowds were astonished at his teaching, for he taught them as one who had authority, and not as their scribes.

(Matt. 7:24–29)

Jesus concludes the most famous sermon ever spoken with a brief, unforgettable parable. This parable is really two stories told side by side. (The parable of the prodigal son is also such a parable with two stories told together, first the journey of a younger son and then the journey of an older son.) The key to the interpretation of a two-story parable is to look closely for the parts of the story narrative that are identical in each story and those parts of the story narrative that are different.

In this parable, notice those elements that are identical: In each story, each person is a *house builder.* What does this mean? Each one of us is building our philosophy of life, establishing our values, building houses in which to live our lives. According to the parable Jesus tells, there is no way that we can avoid this house building. Even nondecisions build a house for us that we must live with. The student who cannot decide about the school musical tryouts has in reality made a decision by that avoidance nondecision. As a result he or she missed the tryout deadline and, therefore, will be living throughout the spring semester in a house that does not include play practice, rehearsals, cast parties, audience reaction, etc.

There is really no such thing as a nondecision that suspends the movement of time and history; and, therefore, we must live in the nondecision houses we build just as we live in the decision houses we build. Indeed, we are all house builders. This possibility is not seen by Jesus as a variable.

A second constant in the two stories that Jesus tells has to do with the storm. Every house we build will face a storm. The sentence that tells of the rain, the floods, and the winds is identical in each parallel account. By this exact repetition, Jesus makes it clear to his listeners that he is not teaching a parable about how to build our houses in a place where there are no storms. This is a parable about foundations and not about weather avoidance. This is not a teaching about the search for a safe context or setting in which to grow a family or a philosophy of life—that ideal atmosphere where the climate is supportive and non-threatening. Jesus has made it clear that every house we build must be able to endure the less-than-ideal climate. In another parable, the parable of the wheat and the weeds, he makes the same point (Matt. 13:24–30). The wheat must grow alongside the weeds until the time of the harvest. The special request for ideal growing conditions is rejected in that parable as the farm workers ask the owner if he plans to pull up the weeds: "No . . . Let both grow together. . . ." As Jesus comes to the close of the Sermon on the Mount, he alerts each of us to hear his words. We must prepare the houses we are building for wind, rain, and floods. We must prepare the child for the road, not the road for the child. There is a testing of all of the houses we are building, and that testing is built into the whole plan; no favorites are excused from the inevitable testing of the value systems and philosophies of life and dreams into which we invest our lives. The variable in the parable is the foundation upon which the house is built.

Two Major Conclusions

This is not a parable about finding a protective environment in which to make it easier for our children to grow up. It is instead a parable about establishing a house that is able to withstand storms. The parable teaches us to prepare the house for the stress of the hurricane rather than to find the neighborhood without the possibility of hurricanes. What is different in the stories is the foundation. From that variable, we discover the principal theological and discipleship teaching of the parable; and as the parable is the summation of the sermon, this teaching becomes a convergent point for the great themes of the sermon itself.

This convergence of themes teaches us two major conclusions. First, the parable is fundamentally a Messianic parable about the all-sufficiency of Jesus Christ himself as the fulfillment of the human search for foundation. He is the adequate foundation for our lives. "Every one then who hears these words of mine and does them will be like a wise man. . . ." Jesus has made himself and his words that Rock, the "Amen" we are to wisely trust. The crowd of people at the lakeside who heard the sermon did not miss this obvious Messianic-fulfillment language: ". . . the crowds were astonished at his teaching, for he taught them as one who had authority. . . ."

Jesus has posed a profound question to all who hear these words. If I do not choose to trust my life to his words, and to his character which sustains those words, then what do I propose to build my life upon? Will the foundation that I choose be able to support the house in the nighttime hurricane as well as in the summer evening? Jesus' parable has forced the question out into the open.

Secondly, the parable is also a story about faith and the freedom choices we make. The parable argues from effect to cause and makes the case that since everything in life is tested we, therefore, need to choose wisely what it is we shall trust. The parable has a point of view that is affirmed by the Teacher. When we have trusted in the words of the Teacher and the Teacher himself, we have trusted in the One who is faithful.

The Lord of the Sermon—Our Foundation

The words of Jesus are called rock, and such an image serves as the "Amen" to the Sermon. The Hebrew word *Amen* is directly related to "foundation" and always has to do in the Old Testament with the faithfulness of God and our human trust in his faithfulness. That faithfulness is now personified before our very eyes as the Teacher of this sermon. Therefore, we may wisely build upon his words; we do well to respond to this person. Faith builds upon the foundation and into the foundation.

I live in earthquake country. And the church I serve in Berkeley, California, is next to the campus of the University of California which sits astride the Hayward fault, itself connected to the gigantic San Andreas Fault that stretches from Mexico to Alaska and directly under the city of San Francisco.

Earthquake specialists have pointed up several important facts about home construction in earthquake terrain: A wood structure is ideally suited for the stresses of horizontal land movement, which is the terror of an earthquake, provided that the wood structure is bolted to its foundation. Another discovery is that ¾-inch plywood corner reinforcements that extend the side walls of a house to the foundation will also greatly strengthen a house against the horizontal land movement. What has been found in recent quakes is that the nonbolted home moves a few inches away from its foundation, and that move away from the foundation causes the collapse of the structure. In other words, a safe house is that house which relates as much of the house as possible to its foundation. It not only rests upon a rock; it is built into the rock.

I have often thought of the Golden Gate Bridge in San Francisco as our city's boldest structure in that its great south pier rests directly upon the fault zone of the San Andreas Fault. That bridge is an amazing structure of both flexibility and strength. It is built to sway some twenty feet at the center of its one-mile suspension span. The secret to its durability is its flexibility that enables this sway, but that is not all. By design, every part of the bridge—its concrete roadway, its steel railings, its cross beams—is inevitably related from one welded joint to the other up through the vast cable system to two great towers and two great land anchor piers. The towers bear most of the weight, and they are deeply imbedded into the rock foundation beneath the sea. In other words, the bridge is totally preoccupied with its foundation. This is its secret! Flexibility and foundation. In the Christian life, it is the forgiveness of the gospel that grants us our flexibility; and it is the Lord of the gospel who is our foundation. There is no other.

The true significance of the sermon in the last analysis,

therefore, depends upon the authority of the teacher. Jesus has not allowed us any other option, because his words cannot be separated from him. "Thus the words of the Sermon on the Mount ultimately lead us back to him who uttered them. Its imperatives thus become themselves indicatives." (W. D. Davies, p. 435.) He does not interpret the Law in technical and legalistic ways as did the scribes, who were often required by the people to search for various options and loopholes. He claims to fulfill the Law; this is the radical difference. "Costly grace," wrote Bonhoeffer, ". . . is the kingly rule of Christ, for whose sake a man will pluck out the eye which causes him to stumble. . . . Such grace is *costly* because it calls us to follow, and it is *grace* because it calls us to follow Jesus Christ. . . . It comes as a word of forgiveness to the broken spirit and the contrite heart." [1]

The gospel in the sermon is, in the deepest sense, the preacher himself; more than any collection of the words in the sermon, the good news of the Sermon on the Mount is Jesus the preacher of the sermon. This is what we mean by the term *Messianic*. A text is Messianic when it points the reader toward God's Messiah, the coming One who is Emmanuel, God with us. In this sense the Law of Moses is profoundly Messianic in two important ways: Its ethical purity and grandeur stir our respect and wonder so that we are eager to meet the Lord of the Law. Secondly, the Law so deeply undermines our pride and self-satisfaction that it brings us to its author to resolve the crisis that the Law itself posed to us. The Law in these two ways draws us to Christ.

The Sermon on the Mount has the same function as the Ten Commandments, in that for the same two reasons we are drawn to the Lord of the sermon.

His closing parable shows his wise understanding of the human creature. We are incurable builders, and we continually build houses by rivers. Jesus does not scold us for building; in fact, his parable endorses that instinct. But we must have a reason to build the houses we build. And most of all, a Rock upon which to build.

"The crowds were astonished at this teaching. . . ." The final note in Matthew 7 is not a part of the sermon. Instead, it is Matthew's observation about the reaction of the people to Jesus. That astonishment the people felt then has continued into our century. Jesus Christ wins us to himself. And it happens to us as we read the words of this sermon, words that are salty and words that are friendly at the same time. Either way, this Teacher wins our respect; and for many people throughout the generations since a crowd was first astonished at Galilee, this sermon has been the beginning of a journey toward the Teacher of the sermon.

NOTES

Introduction
1. W. D. Davies, *The Setting of the Sermon on the Mount* (Cambridge: Cambridge University Press, 1964), 1.
2. Martin Dibelius, *The Sermon on the Mount* (New York: Charles Scribners, 1940), 143.
3. John F. Walvoord, *Matthew, Thy Kingdom Come* (Chicago: Moody Press, 1974), 46.

Chapter 1
1. J. R. R. Tolkien, *The Two Towers* (Boston: Houghton-Mifflin, 1967), 408.
2. G. K. Chesterton, *The Everlasting Man* (New York: Doubleday, 1974), 194, 195.
3. *Theological Dictionary of the New Testament,* Vol. 4 (Grand Rapids: Eerdmans, 19), 362.
4. James Barr, *Biblical Words for Time.* (London: scm, 1962), 263.

Chapter 2
1. William F. Albright and C. S. Mann, *Matthew, The Anchor Bible* (New York: Doubleday, 1971), 55.

Chapter 3
1. Dietrich Bonhoeffer, *Letters and Papers from Prison* (New York: Macmillan, 1972), 5.

2. C. S. Lewis, *Miracles* (New York: Macmillan, 1947), 133.
3. For a further discussion of this, see the author's *Salvation by Surprise* (Waco, Texas: Word, 1975), 21f.
4. Blaise Pascal, *Pensées* (New York: Penguin, 1966), 66, 147.
5. Walter Brueggeman, *The Creative Word* (Philadelphia: Fortress, 1982), 10.
6. Brevard S. Childs, *The Book of Exodus* (Philadelphia: Westminster, 1974), 384.

Chapter 5
1. Aleksandr Solzhenitsyn, *From Under the Rubble* (Boston: Little, Brown, 1974), 136.

Chapter 6
1. C. S. Lewis, *The Screwtape Letters* (New York: Macmillan, 1964), 46.
2. Paul Tournier, *Secrets* (New York: Pillar, 1976), 22.
3. Ibid., 29.

Chapter 7
1. Joachim Jeremias, *New Testament Theology* (New York: Charles Scribners, 1971), 98.
2. James H. Moulton, and George Milligan, *A Vocabulary of the Greek New Testament* (Grand Rapids: Eerdmans, 1949), 242.

Chapter 14
1. Bonhoeffer, *The Cost of Discipleship* (New York: Macmillan, 1963), 211.
2. Ibid., 45–47.
3. Bonhoeffer, *Letters and Papers,* 123.
4. Earl Palmer, *Love Has Its Reasons* (Waco, Texas: Word, 1977), 29.
5. A. M. Hunter, *Teaching and Preaching the New Testament* (Philadelphia: Westminster, 1963), 64.

Chapter 15
1. Bonhoeffer, *Discipleship,* 47, 48.

BIBLIOGRAPHY

Albright, W. F., and Mann, C. S. *Matthew, The Anchor Bible.* New York: Doubleday, 1971.

Allen, W. C. *Matthew,* International Critical Commentary. Edinburgh: T. & T. Clark, 1907.

Argyle, A. W. *The Gospel of Matthew.* Cambridge: Cambridge University Press, 1963.

Barr, James. *Biblical Words for Time.* London: SCM. Press, 1962.

- - - -. *The Semantics of Biblical Language.* Oxford: Oxford University Press, 1961.

Barth, Karl. *Dogmatics in Outline.* New York: Harper and Row, 1959.

Bonhoeffer, Dietrich. *The Cost of Discipleship.* New York: Macmillan, 1963.

Childs, Brevard S. *The Book of Exodus.* Philadelphia: Westminster Press, 1974.

Chrysostom, St. John. *Homilies on the Sermon on the Mount.* Edited by Jaroslov Pelikan. Philadelphia: Fortress Press, 1967.

Davies, W. D. *The Setting of the Sermon on the Mount.* Cambridge: Cambridge University Press, 1964.

Dibelius, Martin. *The Sermon on the Mount.* New York: Charles Scribners, 1940.

Guelich, Robert A. *The Sermon on the Mount.* Waco, Tex.: Word, 1982.

Harris, Archer, and Waltke, Bruce. *Theological Wordbook of the Old Testament.* Chicago: Moody Press, 1980.

Higgins, A. J. B. *New Testament Essays.* Manchester: Manchester University Press, 1959.

Hill, David. *Greek Words and Hebrew Meanings.* Cambridge: Cambridge University Press, 1967.

Hunter, A. M. *Recent Trends in Johannine Studies.*

- - - -. *Teaching and Preaching the New Testament.* Philadelphia: Westminster Press, 1963.

Lenski, R. C. H. *Interpretation of St. Matthew's Gospel.* Columbus, Ohio: Lutheran Book Concern, 1932.

Luther, Martin. *Commentary on the Sermon on the Mount.* Philadelphia: Lutheran Publication Society, 1892.

Manson, T. W. *Studies in the Gospels and Epistles.* Manchester: Manchester University Press, 1962.

Ogilvie, Lloyd. *Congratulations—God Believes in You!* Waco, Tex.: Word, 1980.

Plummer, Alfred. *Exegetical Commentary on the Gospel According to St. Matthew.* London: Robert Scott, 1909.

Robinson, Theodore H. *The Gospel of Matthew,* Moffatt New Testament Commentary. New York: Doubleday, 1928.

Stott, J. R. W. *Christian Counter-Culture.* Downers Grove, Ill.: InterVarsity Press, 1978.

Walvoord, John F. *Matthew, Thy Kingdom Come.* Chicago: Moody Press, 1974.

Watson, Thomas. *The Lord's Prayer.* Edinburgh: The Banner of Truth Institute, 1965.

Tasker, R. V. G. *The Gospel According to Matthew.* Grand Rapids: Eerdmans, 1961.